STICK HORSES

AND OTHER STORIES OF RANCH LIFE

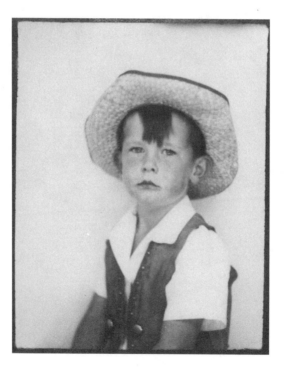

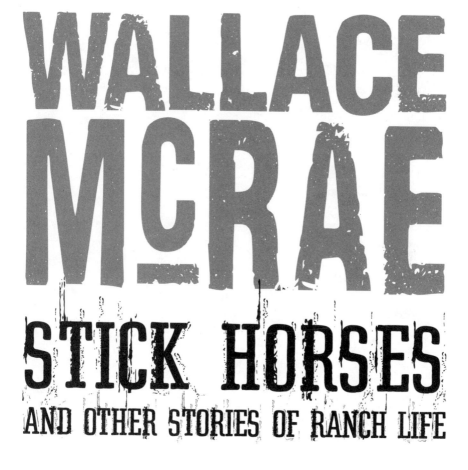

WALLACE McRAE

STICK HORSES

AND OTHER STORIES OF RANCH LIFE

GIBBS SMITH

TO ENRICH AND INSPIRE HUMANKIND

Salt Lake City | Charleston | Santa Fe | Santa Barbara

Published by
Gibbs Smith
P.O. Box 667
Layton, Utah 84041

Orders: 1.800.835.4993
www.gibbs-smith.com

Designed by Debra McQuiston
Printed and bound in the United States of America
Gibbs Smith books are printed on either recycled,
100% post-consumer waste, or FSC-certified papers.

Library of Congress Cataloging-in-Publication Data

McRae, Wallace.
  Stick horses and other stories of ranch life / Wallace McRae. — 1st ed.
    p. cm.
  ISBN-13: 978-1-4236-0591-1
  ISBN-10: 1-4236-0591-8
  1. Ranch life—West (U.S.)—Anecdotes. 2. Cowboys—West (U.S.)—
Social life and customs—Anecdotes. 3. West (U.S.)—Social life and
customs—Anecdotes. 4. McRae, Wallace—Anecdotes. I. Title.
  F596.M147 2009
  978'.033—dc22
                                        2008048502

CONTENTS

PREFACE

Fourteen years ago I died. It's difficult to recall or write about what happened, because much of the time while my death and resurrection were taking place, I was either suffering excruciating pain or partially—or completely—sedated. The events that took place are relevant because they led to the writing of this book.

I won't go into details of my experiencing a heart attack while fencing alone, making it back to the pickup, and driving home to initially find no one there to help me but eventually making it to the Colstrip Medical Clinic. After two vehicular and airborne ambulance rides, I got to the St. Vincent's Hospital in Billings. *That was close,* I thought. *But things are okay now.* Little did I know.

In order to evaluate the damage caused by the heart attack, it is a fairly routine procedure to take a look at the heart's blood vessels using an angiogram. In order to do this, a catheter is inserted into the femoral artery. The tube is threaded into the aorta, then up the aorta to the heart, where dye is squirted in. An X-ray is taken that shows the extent of damage, and the cardiologist then decides how best fix the problem. Apparently there's a pretty tight curve in the aorta jut before you get to the heart, and sometimes the catheter probe runs off the outside of the track and pokes a hole in the artery. Then the patient is in a whole lot of trouble. When the medical team saw my blood pressure take a dive and couldn't detect a pulse, they cracked open my chest and "to hell with the diagnosis; we'll patch the hole—and as long as we're in here, let's just do a quadruple bypass and hope for the best."

I doubt if, at this stage, anyone expected me to recover. Close friends and relatives were called by my wife, Ruth, or son, Clint, who were at the hospital on vigil. Daughters Allison and Natalie came from their homes in Tacoma and Japan, neither expecting me to be alive when they arrived.

My best friend and fellow poet Paul Zarzyski and his partner, Elizabeth Dear, were on their way to visit Paul's parents in Wisconsin when they heard of my condition and were among my first visitors. Clint had to claim Paul as his brother in order for him to qualify as a family member and get into the recovery room to see me. The only sensual facilities I had were sight and hearing. I couldn't talk because of the breathing tube from the respirator running down my windpipe. Paul said I looked awful—well that wasn't the word he used, but you get the idea. "You were bloated like a Tongue River carp left on the riverbank for three days. Your color was like the shade of a sucker's belly from Cominski Crick back in Wisconsin. I counted five tubes coming *out* of various places in your body. You had a urine-colored stain that failed to disguise or camouflage the crudely embroidered sutures on your chest. Wallace, you looked worse than dead."

Although I couldn't reply, I was touched by Paul's pleading. "Wallace, please don't die. I don't know if you can hear me, or if you can do anything to prevent it, but just don't die. If you die, I won't ever want to go on stage and do poems again, without you there beside me or listening in the audience. And you still have too many stories to tell. You have to recover and write them down. You have to write them down."

Later, after I healed up, Paul asked if I remembered his visiting me in the recovery room. "Of course," I said, "I especially remember the part about you never wanting to do your poems again if I died. You have no idea how tempting it was for me do a real service to all of the fans of cowboy poetry by just cashing it all in and riding on over that big divide just to get you to shut the hell up!"

On a more serious note, I added, "I also remember you pleading with me to hang on long enough to write all of the stories I had been telling you over the years. Damn it, Paul, you know I've tried, but I just can't get them to fit in meter and rhyme."

"Forget about meter and rhyme," he said. "Write them just like you tell them. Write them as stories, or essays. Just write them down. Write them as prose, not poetry."

"But I don't know anything about writing prose," I protested.

"You don't know anything about writing poetry, either," Paul said, "but that never held you back. Write those stories of yours as prose."

So that's what I've done. If you don't like it, talk to Zarzyski. This was his idea.

STICK HORSES

Nearly every morning one of us would wrangle the horses. Occasionally there was other, more compelling, work to be done, but we preferred to ride. We kept a wrangle horse "up" by picketing him to the gatepost at the back door of our grandparents' house.

As was the case with the ones we rode, we rotated the wrangle horse. Not all members of the cavvy were fit to ride to gather the rest, however. Some were afflicted with defects—a fistula, cinch sore or wire cut. Some were packing just a bit too much of that hot Thoroughbred blood crazying them up, so using them for running in the other horses rendered them mentally unfit to ride for weeks. Some were either permanently or temporarily unsound. Some were not sufficiently broken and considered too green for the job.

Our wrangle pasture was defined by the decorative twisted and woven wire fence, its top domed and scalloped like cathedral windows. The wire was stapled to juniper and pitch pine posts, enclosing the yard at the larger of two ranch homes.

Our shared grandfather was the only adult on the ranch who understood, and believed, our remuda to be comprised of *real* horses. They most definitely were not mere stick horses. From his rocking chair on the screened porch, Grandpa would watch us wrangle. He understood what we were doing and probably didn't approve, though he never spoke of it. The blood meandering through his ever-weakening heart to his ever-decreasing brain cells was more inclined to cause him to favor the sheep and black-and-white collie dogs of earlier years than cattle and horses. Our feelings about our grandfather were comprised of a mixture of mild fear and slight revulsion. We feared that which we did not understand. We were mystified by his mumbled words and purposeless wanderings. We were repulsed by his scents of sour breath, sweat and soiled woolen underwear. While he didn't talk directly to us, he was not silent. Once, when we were intensely focused upon a bull snake swallowing two hen's eggs from a nest hidden behind the latticework under the porch, Grandpa slipped up behind us in his noiseless sheepskin slippers and loudly said, "Umpaugh-paugh!" scaring the bejesus out of both of us.

After wrangling, we would each select our mount for the day. This decision required a great deal of consideration and was never a hasty one. The wrangler might, for instance, report that during the gather it was discovered that "Cedar" or that buckskin "Willow" or even "Hard Ash" appeared to be a bit lame. Of course, we couldn't ride them until they were once again judged to be sound. We considered whose turn it was in the rotation and "who needed rode." The final decision was also based on the purpose of the ride, which was a result of much palaver and negotiation before arriving at a mostly mutual agreement.

Sometimes we rode purely for pleasure, selecting a well-broke, easy-traveling mount upon which to get the mail, to gather the eggs in a small galvanized bucket, to ride up and wrestle the lid off the black cast-iron kettle and sniff the fermenting barley for the hogs, or to assay the garden for ripe tomatoes or sufficiently sized cucumbers, which we delivered to both houses in the egg bucket.

If it were to be a serious ride, we would choose something to fit the task. A big circle, gathering either imaginary wild cattle (or wild sticks) to replenish gaps in the cavvy, would dictate the selection of a big, stout, "all heart, no brains" rough ash or gate-stick-sized pitch pine that would ooze pungent "snot" or "sweat" into your left palm as you rode. If "working the herd" was the order of the day, a supple, limber, lightning-quick willow was selected.

We had a few "show"—or more accurately "show-off"— steeds for those rare opportunities when company or relatives from Back East (which meant from any place east of Miles City or west of Billings) were expected. One of these show horses was a length of milled quarter-round left in the salt house, a remnant of some long-forgotten carpenter's construction—a "Quarter Horse" in our nomenclature, but more of the frail Arab-type in reality. Another was a straight-grained juniper that we had pared to its rich sorrel core with a forbidden drawknife. We both loved "Cedar" and each spring would curry and shed a winter's coat of gray by sanding it on the sickle-sharpening grindstone, which we peddled in turns. Our favorite? A classy diamond willow we acquired by devious means. Both Carol and I coveted and loved "Diamond," and his contentious ownership was finally resolved in my favor by consenting to be examined after having dropped my overalls and underdrawers for her close and complete inspection.

Annually, in late July or early August, we would run in a fresh herd of "green horses" to break. They were gathered from various ranges, but their favorite haunts were behind the blacksmith shop, on the south side of the chicken house and at the base of the steep winter-sledding hill where the hog pasture fell off towards the creek. After a rain, which made gathering easier, we would ride a couple of stout circle horses into the green horse range. After circling and holding up the gather, we would dismount, ground tie our broke horses and begin to "work the herd" on the tall, broad-leafed horse weeds, pulling them from the manure-rich ground by their roots. It was hard, physically demanding work made even more so due to the fact that both Carol and I suffered from hay fever and were especially allergic to horseweed pollen. With binder twine, we tied in a slipknot around their thick necks. "It don't matter if a few choke plumb to death; the range is full of 'em," we'd say, as we tied them up to the heavy steel swiveled ring set in the concrete wall of the barn's lower floor. Once we were satisfied that they had learned not to pull back, we would proceed to "rough 'em up and sack 'em out." As we pruned the large leaves from the stalk, using a discarded rusty serrated mower sickle section, we would slap them with the leaves until they became accustomed to the new stimulus and quit flinching. The manes (long, tangled root hairs) and tails (allergy-inducing flower tassels) were left untrimmed and ragged, befitting the wild, unbroken state of these green broncs. While one "eared the bronc" the other would gingerly climb aboard trembling with fear, bravado and adrenalin for that first ride. "Turn him loose!" the rider would shout and go off on a wild, flatulent ride that resulted in either an eventual runaway or a bone-crunching buck off. It bothered me that Carol was the better roughstock rider. Perhaps it was genetic. Her father was superior to my dad forking a bronc, but there was some consolation in the fact that my horses handled better and were faster than hers.

★　★　★

Although I've quizzed family members, Cheyenne Reservation residents and neighbors about her real name, my inquiries have proven to be inconclusive. A few have thought her name might have been Bessie Crooked Nose. If this is the case, I doubt that Carol or I ever knew it. Because of her limping, walking-stick-aided gait, we called her "Tippy Toe."

Had we lived along a railroad, or a paved road, such as the Yellowstone Highway on the south side of the river by the county seat, fifty dirt-road miles away, she would have been considered a female hobo. Instead she was merely a grub line rider, or a bum. She would work the ranches and grocery-carrying general stores looking for food. I'm unsure as to how she made her rounds. I speculate that she caught a ride with the kindly stage driver, Emmett Boslaugh, on his trips to the Forsyth post office and the Cheyenne Reservation Agency in Lame Deer. Despite living with the Cheyennes, I'm not sure she was a member of the local tribe. Apparently she had no permanent home or family to help with her basic needs. Had she been Cheyenne, their cultural tradition of respect and caring for their elders would have prevented her having to live off handouts. She may have been Sioux. The close alliance between that tribe and the Cheyennes could explain her presence in our area. She communicated in the Cheyenne language, understood some English, but did not, to my knowledge, speak it.

Tippy Toe was quite discriminate in her begging. Many of our neighbors have no recollection of her. Ours was apparently the only ranch in the immediate neighborhood where she would periodically drop by for a handout. My mother, or Carol's, must have baked bread on a certain set day of the week because Tippy Toe would show up regularly on baking day.

When Carol or I detected Tippy Toe slowly gimping down the lane from the mailbox, we had ample time to catch and mount fast horses, ride up and circle this wrinkled, blanketed, moccasined beggar as she approached. While fascinated by her, we were equally as wary of her as of a great gray bear or one of the wolves so hated by our grandfather. We knew, you see. We lived along the creek traveled by Custer and the 7th on their way to the Little Horn. We knew what happened to them. We knew who did it. We knew that Indians were godless savages that scalped innocent victims and, if they thought they could get away with it, kidnapped small white children and forced them to become either slaves or Indians. So we approached Tippy Toe with both fear and fascination while mounted on quick, ears-up, skittish, snorting, shying steeds.

Reining in, we would follow Tippy Toe at a safe distance, observing, as she limped along, that the toe of her right moccasin was worn through, while the heel, never touching the ground, was barely scuffed. Choosing the back steps of one of our homes, Tippy Toe would settle herself until discovered by some responsible adult. My cousin and I, keeping a safe distance from, and a vigil with, the old woman, would wait. If no adult appeared, she would arthritically rise and enter the house to slowly and quietly wander around examining and admiring its contents until finally, satisfied with her reconnaissance, settling into a comfortable chair. Once she hand-rolled a cigarette and struck a match on the wooden arm of the chair, leaving a permanent scorch scar. As she sat, she would often smile at us and whisper words as incomprehensible as those of Grandpa, and maybe hum a dissonant tune. We three would wait. And watch.

Most times, however, she was discovered as she waited on the back steps of the ranch house. "*Hy yaw!*" she would say and nod in a rocking bow. "*Hy yaw.*" Then "*Veho' kok' en hy ya,*" which meant "bread." After the crusty home-baked bread was delivered a whole loaf at a time to her surprisingly smooth, unwrinkled hands, "*k'Oy umsk!*" ("butter") she'd demand. A huge bowl of freeform butter, yellow as the summer sun and sweating with beads of clear buttermilk that only endless hand working could eliminate, would be delivered. From under her cotton blanket, worn over her head as a scarf and wrapped around her body, she would produce a curved-blade skinning knife, beveled on only one side, with a stained copper-riveted wooden handle. She would carve off a huge slab of bread, then before buttering or eating a bite, she would tear off a small chunk, mumble some words and toss the morsel over her shoulder—for the Spirits, we learned later.

After she had eaten, picked all the crumbs from her lap with moistened fingertips and rested for a bit, she would rise. Then, taking her walking stick from where it leaned on the yard gatepost, she would—in her rocking, limping, toe-down, heel-up gait—go back up the barbed-wire-fenced lane, past the cut bank along the creek, towards the county road.

One day, after she had eaten and had drunk a blue enamelware cup or two of coffee laced with thick cream and enough sugar so that the remnants had to be salvaged and licked from her index finger, she rose and in retrieving her walking stick saw, at the same instant as Carol and I, that our entire remuda was still in lounging, hipshot by the yard gate. In our haste to meet and escort Tippy Toe, we had forgotten to gather the rest of the remuda in the crook of our right arms and scatter them around the yard where they could water and graze. We had forgotten! Tippy Toe gathered the horses in the crook of her own left arm and we initially assumed she was going to take the responsibility of spreading them about the yard. But no! She began working the herd! Casting aside the wispy cutting horses, the green broncs and any of suspect stamina or with conformational defects, she was sorting into her keeper cut all of our best equines. She paused and smiled at us as she caressed the neck of Carol's prized Cedar, and my beloved Diamond. "*Píva! Ish píva! Ha ho!*" (Good! Very good! Thank you!) she exclaimed. If we had understood, we would have only been impressed by her unerring ability to select for stamina, beauty and quality.

As she started up the hill towards the county road, we ran to Grandpa and simultaneously and hysterically reported to him that our horses had been stolen in an Indian raid. We tried to convince him that with quick and decisive action there was still time to not only prevent a felony and the possible shedding of blood but to rescue the horses!

"Umpaugh paugh," Grandpa said, as he playfully poked his pointing finger into our tummies.

Having come to understand that Grandpa had been raised under a strict Scottish Presbyterian code and had never uttered a swear word in his entire life, I boldly decided to go for broke and hopefully shock him into action. "Dammit to hell, Grandpa, the bastard sonofabitch stole our horses!" I screamed to Carol's amazement. "Umpaugh . . . paugh . . . ," Grandpa said.

We flying-mounted a couple of the remnants of our remuda and, cutting below the chicken house and behind the hog house and shop, raced to head Tippy Toe off at the narrow spot in the lane against the cut bank. We made it with time to spare. Panting and petting our steeds on the neck to settle and reassure them, we waited to confront our enemy.

We stood our ground. She closed the gap. We stood our ground. Suddenly, surprising me as I was about to weaken, Carol dashed in and grabbed for Cedar. Tippy Toe fended Carol off with her own poor excuse of a tired walking-stick horse, greasy and sweat-stained about its neck and head, its unshod hooves quarter cracked and worn to the quick, its barked and tattered hide scarred and flyblown. As we regrouped and prepared for another desperate act, the old Indian woman reached beneath her blanket, retrieved her skinning knife and triumphantly laughed as she slashed it through the air about her as if it were a cavalry saber. We abandoned our horses and ran for home.

After the skirmish with Tippy Toe and the loss of most of our stick horse flesh, we developed other interests. We went through a bow and arrow phase. We declared war on the English sparrows nesting in the barn loft. When we were able to get hooks, we became serious fishers of the creek for the suckers, bullheads and minnows that swam in its warm, murky pools. With the help of a Rat Terrier, "Dewey," and a papered Newfoundland, "Cappy," we became nearly professional cat chasers. But our stick horse days were over. Maybe we just outgrew that particular game.

Decades later, after Carol was killed in an automobile accident, I asked her father, my Uncle Evan, about Tippy Toe and why she was indulged and fed on our ranch. I wished that I had queried my parents or my aunt, since they were more inclined to lend insight into answering my question, but they, like my grandfather, had died by that time. In his curt, decisive manner, however, my uncle's explanation put that, and many other unasked questions, into perspective and context. He said, "I don't know. I guess we sort of inherited that poor old woman. This country of ours used to be theirs. We got it after our government took it away from them. My dad, your grandpa, got squeezed and starved out in Scotland. Your other grandpa was in the cavalry. Maybe we felt we owed her in some way. It's hard to say, but the reason she limped was because she had her heel shot off by a .45-70 bullet from a cavalry rifle at, I think, the Battle of Wounded Knee, when she was about the age of you and Carol back when you used to play stick horses. Maybe that's why. Hell, Wallace, I don't know."

DANGEROUS
DAN IMLAH

The small, frail frame house we lived in had been abandoned by a failed homesteader. My dad recruited a dozen teams of horses from the neighbors to skid it on the snow a couple of miles to our ranch headquarters. When I was four years old, my parents decided it was inadequate. My parents traded the homesteader's house to a sawyer in Lame Deer for the rough structural lumber and logs for a new two-story, Cape Cod–style log home.

The first order of business was to drill a well for the house. Dad recruited and consulted Dan Imlah, who owned a hardscrabble bachelor outfit on the Little Porcupine and was the local well driller. My parents were partial, albeit uncommitted, believers in divining, or "witching" for water using a forked willow stick. "Know how to find good water?" my Dad asked the driller.

"Uhuh," Dan replied in his usual surly manner.

"Will you witch for it?"

Dan snorted, adding, "I find it by digging. I'll be here in a week or so . . . if I feel like it. Drive a stick in the ground where you want it."

"You'll case off the surface hard water won't you?" Dad asked.

"I'll do as I damn please. But I'll get you a well," Dan said and drove off as if offended by the prospect of a job.

True to his word, a week or so later he came clattering down the lane herding the most fascinating truck-mounted collection of junk that my young eyes had ever seen. I watched with amazement as the derrick was raised over the selected spot and Dan began scattering pipes and tools all over the flat.

"You stay away from the well rig, you hear? It is dangerous work and Dan does not like people. Especially kids," my mother ordered. I knew she wasn't kidding. "They call him 'Dangerous Dan,'" she added, and gave me a grown-up, knowing look.

I couldn't help it. The activity, noise and intricate machinery were just too great an attraction to resist. I didn't approach this mysterious but fascinating man. I didn't say anything when there was a cessation of the noise and activity, but I set up my observation post about fifty feet away. And I watched.

★ ★ ★

Dan stayed in our bunkhouse and ate with us. The third day of the drilling, he walked by me on his way to wash up and eat the noon meal. He hadn't looked my way that I knew of, nor did he look at me as he walked by, but he asked in a civil way, "Want to know how deep I've drilled?"

I was taken by surprise but managed to mumble out, "No."

"Every other son of a bitch always wants to know. Why don't you?"

"I don't know. I just like to watch," I said.

During the heat of the next day, Dan looked at me directly and asked, "You got a name, kid?"

"Wallace."

"Wallace, take this water bag down to the windmill and get me some fresh cool water." When I got back with the water,

I set the canvas water bag on a rock while keeping my usual distance. "Bring it over here and I won't have to shut the rig down," he yelled over the noise of the unmuffled engine. My mother, hearing him shout, came out of the house.

"I'm not supposed to," I hollered back.

He shut down the engine and came over to me, picked up the bag and drank deeply. Water ran down his chin and neck and mixed with the sweat on his faded blue chambray shirt. He backed off about ten yards and sat down. We talked. I don't remember what we talked about. It's been over sixty years and it doesn't matter. My mother went back in the house.

A couple of days later, he left. We had a new well with sweet, soft water. The surface water seams had been sealed out. After Dan left, my dad said, "Dan said that you were a nice boy."

"I think he's a nice man," I said, "I don't think he's dangerous."

"Who knows," my dad said.

★　★　★

Decades later, after I had been away to college and the navy, an unshaven, shabby old crippled man came up to me one day while I was in the lobby of the Joseph Hotel waiting for my wife to finish shopping in Forsyth. "Are you Wallace?" he asked. I nodded. "I'm 'Dangerous Dan,'" he said, "I drilled a well for your folks one time. You probably don't remember."

"I remember," I said, "I was afraid of you, but you were my friend."

"You're the only kid I ever liked," he said.

HEAD, HEART, HANDS & HEALTH

Cub and Boy Scouts, Campfire Girls, Little League Baseball and other youth activities designed primarily for urban kids have their place, I guess. My mind is not made up on the merits of Demolay, Job's Daughters and Rainbow Girls and their ilk (although I spent a portion of my dissolute youth in an unsuccessful attempt to discover at which end of the latter lay the pot of gold). But, by George, we rural kids had 4-H! Take that, you city elitists!

The smart advice in project selection has always been "follow the money; feed a steer." Forget about the hogs, sheep, breeding heifers and horses. Feed the steer to near foundering and hope the local grocer, or grandpa, will pay big bucks for the beast at the annual Fat Stock Sale at the county fair. It's a competitive event that brings out the worst in people, I believe. As my dad would say while selecting bulls, "Fat's a good color." He did not mean it as a compliment.

This is not feeding country. Even with outstanding olfactory ability you would be hard-pressed to sniff out a genuine fat cattle–producing feedlot. The vast majority of us are livestock producers, not feeders. Oh, there is a good portion of cattlemen running steers or, maybe, spayed heifers, but those cattle graze on grass and then, in the fall, are sold to those folks with the hammer loops on the starboard leg of their bibs—the feeders. That's the way it works. Don't tell me that the kid is trying to get college money by bucketing corn or barley to some obese bovine lout. It's a violation of the Cowboy Code.

Both of my sisters were deeply involved in 4-H. For years, they participated in some very worthwhile projects: sewing, cooking and other girl enterprises. Beyond being involved in these basic skills, they were also encouraged by my parents to become comfortable in public speaking by participating in "demonstrations."

When I became of age, it was decided I should be involved in the local club as well. "What do you want to do for your main project?" I was asked.

I was only ten years old, but I knew the deal. "I guess I'll feed a fat steer," I proposed. The only experience I had with penned livestock was with the milk cows' calves. My cousin and I had futilely attempted to ride them with a short section from a broken lariat for a surcingle.

"What are you going to use for feed?" my dad asked.

"Grain?"

"We don't raise grain," he pointed out, "Where are you going to get it?"

"We feed the chickens wheat and the pigs some barley," I suggested in what I knew was probably a losing argument. "Maybe I could feed him wheat. Bradleys thresh and have lots of it. Maybe they could sell us enough more wheat to feed my steer."

Bringing up the chickens was a mistake. "Why don't you raise the chickens, then," my mother, ever the arbitrator and conciliator, suggested.

A few weeks later, Emmett Boslaugh, the stage driver, delivered a flat, ventilated cardboard box containing one hundred fuzzy, yellow, unsexed chicks. Most of them were still alive. I became a chicken farmer for the ranch families, the 4-H, the president of the United States and maybe even God. I fed them clabbered milk. I ground Bradleys' wheat in a hand grinder and made mash. I carefully crushed eggshells (so the chickens would not recognize the source and become "egg eaters"). I kept them supplied with fresh water, made sure they were all inside and confined each night, and I loved them.

Anyone who has not ordered randomly selected chicks by mail would logically assume that half would be pullets and half pre-pubescent roosters. Correct? The free market system and capitalism dictate, however, that since laying hens are more monetarily productive than roosters, what the unsuspecting consumer actually receives is long to cockerels. I don't know how they judge the sex of the chicks when they are only a day or so old, but the hatcheries have a system that works and I don't even want to contemplate how they do it. I didn't care. In fact, the teenage roosters were much more entertaining as they developed than the more docile hens.

My poultry project was not without personal tragedy. One day, a sudden violent wind blew over a heavy wooden panel and smashed fourteen of my babies. Not counting the initial DOAs in the delivery box, I had only lost three others to undiagnosed causes. Since "nothing goes to waste on the farm," the gallant fourteen were fed to the hogs. My grief was akin to those greedy fat steer feeders who sell their charges at the fair prior to their slaughter. However, unlike them, I received no monetary compensation, or consolation, for my loss.

One day as fall approached, my mother showed me a bunch of blue-colored, key ring-shaped celluloid rings. "Tonight we are going to catch your roosters while they are on their roosts. We'll put them in the brooder house and butcher them tomorrow. Now, I know you have some special rooster friends, so today if you want to save a few of them, catch them and put one of these rings on their leg. Okay?"

It was not okay, but there was no room for negotiation. It was not an easy job, but by nightfall I had managed to catch every rooster in my herd and decorate their leg with a blue celluloid ring. The next day mother packed me a lunch. My dad caught Snooper, and I spent the day suffering and aimlessly riding the countryside. That evening, I still had my hens and three roosters.

During the summer of that year, most of the kids in the county retreated to Crazy Head Springs on the Cheyenne reservation for 4-H Camp. We escaped summer's heat for a spell in the pine-forested higher elevation. We made new friends. We participated in mundane crafts. The girls stayed in the dormitory built by the CCC boys during the Depression years and we all ate in the log mess hall. On the last night of the camp, we all gathered around a campfire and some of us were designated to participate in a ceremony highlighting our particular project. I was given a chunk of firewood to add to the bonfire and a short script extolling my particular project which I read to the assembly: "This fagot is for poultry, which gives us eggs for our breakfast and wholesome meat for our families' tables." I suppose the whole experience was one of learning, but "this fagot is for poultry . . ." is a line I hope all of the attendees but me have forgotten over the years. Maybe that's why I'm somewhat ambivalent, to this day, about the merits of kids participating in 4-H.

That was the end of my 4-H project featuring farm animals, but 4-H was not quite through with me. Hazel Thompson, the county extension agent, stumbled across what she considered to be an extremely cute idea. Hazel had heard of a boys-only club somewhere back East devoted exclusively to cooking projects. She approached my sister Marjorie and convinced her to be our junior leader, a position practically guaranteeing Marjorie a trip to Chicago to the International 4-H Club Congress. My buddies and I were quickly whipped into shape as members of the Gingerbread Boys Club.

The next summer at camp, a teenage boy asked me what major projects I had been involved in.

"Chickens and cooking," I answered.

"You poor kid," he said.

TOILET BIRDS

Roger Tory Peterson, who wrote the definitive *Field Guide to Western Birds,* would not approve, but we were unrestrained by experts when naming some of our local avian friends. Their nighthawk was our bullbat, probably due to its bull-like snort while zooming—bat-like—around the sky at dusk, catching insects in flight. "Bullbat," while not particularly complimentary, was more kind than it could have been had we noted their tendency to sit stupidly in the middle of the county road committing suicide from being hit by even slow-moving traffic and named them accordingly. The ornithologist's kestrel was our sparrow hawk. Sharp-tail grouse were prairie chickens and sage grouse were sage hens, whatever the sex of the bird. Blue herons were blue cranes. Cliff swallows were mud daubers. We wouldn't have recognized a pinion pine if a logger misjudged the wind and allowed one to fall on us, so their pinion jays were our pine crows.

Our equally misinformed neighbors shared the same regional mistakes in the nomenclature of our flying friends with feathers. With one exception: we had toilet birds. Our neighbors either did not, or would not, admit to having them.

If they had been named for their unsanitary bodily elimination characteristics, the blue cranes who whitewashed acres of ground and brush under their rookeries in tall cottonwood trees or the hated English sparrows would have been likely candidates for the toilet bird label. Our toilet birds not only exhibited clean personal habits but were somewhat sleek and handsome as well. The uninformed might mistake them for smallish robins whose breasts were bleached to a pale orange. When excited, unlike robins, they sprouted a small crest on their poll. Grubbing for worms was most certainly beneath their sense of propriety as they flitted about catching millers and other flying prey. Although I am guilty of describing them in anthropomorphic terms, they were kind, pleasant, courteous, and exhibited a pleasing laissez-faire attitude toward humans.

Our toilet birds built their nests in our outhouses. Thus their name. We shared a symbiotic relationship with them. They enjoyed both shelter and access—through gaps between the rafters—while we were the beneficiaries of their ability and inclination to catch flying insects that frequented the outhouse. The nesting and incubating pair would become accustomed to the comings, doings and goings of us humans. By the time their usual family of four hatchlings came along, we were accepted visitors in their domain. Oh, they might fuss about a bit, protesting with a plaintive, tonally descending *peeew*, which in bird lingo translates to "don't mess with our babies." We respected them. Parents warned us kids to not touch their eggs or babies, which could, even for small children, be reached by standing on the seat of the outhouse. If kids failed to heed this rule, the adult birds would "abandon their nests, eggs or babies and move someplace else where their rights would be respected by more thoughtful and well-behaved children."

In our attempts to emulate those fictitious well-behaved child examples, we learned to avoid various words and references. Defecation was called "going boom" or "making a bone." Urination was referred to as "going chair-chair." In deference to polite society, the term *toilet birds* was discouraged. The fact that our homes finally became "electrified" and enjoyed running water, including indoor bathroom facilities, made the term *toilet birds* obsolete. We were no longer reminded of the birds several times a day as we shared their summer homes.

While I was much too young to appreciate its contents, my bird-loving maternal grandmother, Minnie McKay, presented me with a magnificently illustrated book, *Birds of America*. For a while, the major use of the book was as a booster enabling me to be seated at the dinner table in an adult chair. In time, I began to seriously study the pictures, and upon learning to read, the names of many of the familiar birds. Imagine my surprise at finding our beloved toilet birds had another, more acceptable, name. They were Say's Phoebes.

One of the college courses I studied was ornithology, taught by Dr. Cliff Davis. Dr. Davis was an enthusiastic, engaging and interesting instructor. His field trips displayed not only his love of birds, which was transferred to his students, but his marvelous ability at species identification.

Dr. Davis' grading system relied exclusively on "station tests." From his seemingly endless supply, he would place a series of preserved, stuffed bird skins—complete with beaks and feet—on tables, with a stool in front of each specimen. We were given a brief, timed period at each station to write down the common name and family of each bird. A bell signaled the expiration of time and we moved to the next station. Although I enjoyed the class, the confusion of the damned ducks and the innumerable sparrows placed me precariously balanced with a low C before the final exam, which we students knew would be a frantic review of our entire identification abilities. You will never know how tempted I was when I slid onto the stool before one of my old friends, a toilet bird. I wish I had been in a scholastic position to write down on my test sheet, "Toilet Bird, *Tyrannidae*," instead of "Say's Phoebe, *Tyrannidae*." I suppose the kindly Dr. Cliff Davis might have let me plead my case, and

"ALL THE WORLD'S A STAGE"

I imagine the adults—our two sets of parents, grandfather and assorted hired hands—approved of our willingness to do the job. Our agreeing to retrieve the mail was indication of eagerness to do chores and to assume responsibility. Our older siblings were willing to relinquish the six-days-a-week duty because they had become bored with that job and had moved on to more grown-up and demanding tasks.

Of course, our eagerness had nothing whatsoever to do with work or the assumption of responsibility, although they were part of the deal. "*Now bring the mail straight home. Don't dillydally. Don't lose anything. The mail is important. Don't get the mail wet or dirty. Don't set the sack down for a bit while you throw rocks in the creek. Don't bother the mailman. Straight home, you hear?*"

We heard and heeded various adult admonitions on the same theme. Because getting the mail was exciting. Although it wasn't the best show in town—we lived fifty miles out in the country—it was the best show on the ranch, because the stage driver, Emmett Boslaugh, knew that he was center stage, down front, in a daily dramatic comedy show, and he played his part to the hilt.

Getting the mail was not our only diversion. We had other forms of entertainment. There was a tall, cabinet-style wind-up Victrola on the front porch of Carol's parents' house. If the older kids weren't around to boss us, we would gather up a few 78 rpm records (Sir Harry Lauder's were our favorites) and a dining room chair to climb on so we could set the records on the pool table–green felt turntable and reach the on/off and speed controls. We would jockey for the right to crank up the spring. The loser of the wind-up competition was anointed with the opportunity to flip the lever to "ON," carefully rotate the needle carrier down to the shiny surface of the record and move the speed control from "F" to "S" as it suited the operator. We could barely understand Harry Lauder's broad Scottish accent at normal speeds. We knew that he was funny: the adults laughed at some of his songs and dialog. But to us kids, changing from rapid-fire chirping "Fast" to muffled, bottom-of-the-well "Slow" raised funny to a higher plain of humor. The only thing more entertaining for us was to play "A Wee Dunkin Dorris," which had a scratch about a third of the way in from the outside. Poor Sir Harry would be muddling along, "Just a wee dunkin dorris, just a wee one, wee one, wee one, wee one, wee one . . . ," which we thought was hilarious, especially on the "F" speed setting, until someone would put an end to our fun by screaming, for no apparent reason, "*You kids turn that thing off and get way away from it!*"

We would conduct matched claiming horse races on the sloped tongue-and-groove floor of the same porch that held the Victrola. Each of us would carefully select a marble racehorse from our draw-stringed, once-white muslin marble bag and put it into a device that some might dismiss as merely an upside-down, wooden Kraft cheese box, but to us was the "starting gate." With both of us making sure that the back of the starting gate was flush with the inside porch wall, the starter (which was decided by a complicated procedure of guessing the color of several hand-held marbles) would rotate the downslope side of the starting gate upwards. The horses would race down the splintery fir track, with much boisterous cheering and plaintive urging on the part of their owners, to the 2" x 4" floor plate "finish line." The owner of the winning marble claimed the loser's. Our luck, and resultant quantities of horseflesh marbles, would ebb and flow. I once had a black-and-white swirl that, for reasons beyond recall, was named "Brother Rat" that once nearly put the whining, complaining, protesting Carol out of the racehorse business until one fateful day Brother Rat stumbled and veered off sideways after hitting a box elder bug leg that I had failed to see and therefore remove from the track prior to the running of the race. After losing nearly all of my horses back to Brother Rat and his new owner, Carol, I snookered her into agreeing to what I called a "Blind Jockey Race," where neither of us could see the other's entry until the starting gate opened. I entered a "ringer," of course, in the form of a ball bearing "steelie" that was usually forbidden in all other marble games. My "Silver" started fast and never looked back, and over her howling protests to the disinterested race stewards (her parents), Brother Rat was once again in my stable.

After that, our marble horse racing days were over. My cousin Carol had a vast herd of mostly jug heads, and I was left with just a small remuda, which, to my insufferable pride, included the veteran Brother Rat and the unbeatable Silver. She seemed satisfied with sheer numbers but wasn't willing to risk them. I was happy with the quality of my cavvy.

We had other forms of entertainment involving marbles. One of those was "riding, gathering and working cattle." Normal children played with marbles much differently than Carol and I did. They would draw a ring in the dirt, use the larger marbles as "shooters" and knock other marbles out of the ring. If the players were playing "for keeps," which was the only logical way to play, since it was prohibited on the school grounds, the shooter kept any marbles that were shot out of the ring using a bigger marble as a thumb-knuckled cue ball. We tried this game a few times but derived no great satisfaction from it, perhaps because it was a "town" game that didn't involve imagined livestock. And, frankly, neither of us was very good at it.

When we were racing, the bigger "shooters" were not used. They were considered "work," or "draft," horses and therefore much slower than the smaller "running" horses. When we were "riding, gathering and working cattle," however, the shooters became saddle horses and the smaller marbles were cattle. First, using wooden blocks, we would build a set of corrals. There would be a great deal of considering to do before the actual construction began. "How many pens ya think we oughta have?" one of us would ask.

"Enough to hold all the cuts," the other would answer.

"Well, how many cuts do you figger?"

If no one was listening, "Hell, you're doin' it," was the answer.

"Where ya want the penning gate?"

"Away from the sun. They won't go in there for poop (one of our favorite words) into the sun."

"Well, where's the sun then?"

"In the sky, last I looked, but let's pretend that it's over by the front window, and it's morning, so put it on the end towards the window."

"Where should we gather the cattle from?"

"Just the parlor, the dining room and the front room. Mama doesn't want them in the kitchen. Last time we rode she almost fell down on an old crippled red-necked bull we missed."

Once the cattle were scattered in the various "pastures," we would mount up and, working from the outside of the rooms, begin bumping the "cattle" into bunches using the "horses" and pushing them towards the corral. "Keep 'em narrow."

"*I am* keeping them narrow."

"Watch that green son of a bitch tryin' to git away."

"You're the one mashed him out. Don't yell at me."

"You kids quit fighting in there or you'll have to go outside."

"Yes, Mama. Now *see*. It's your fault."

"I mean it. Quit it!"

"Yes, Mama."

Sometimes we would work the cattle in the corral. More often we would work them outside, corralling each cut as it was worked. It was pretty hard to tell the sex or condition of marbles, so they were sorted by color. "Let's work all of the reds first."

"Okay, how deep you wanta go?"

"Anything that's mostly red, or red with white, or white with red."

"Looks to me like there's less blue ones."

"I don't think so, unless you count the blue-green ones as being green."

"Okay, we'll call the blue-green ones green. But what about that bluish-green one right there with the little bit of red on it?"

"Last time we called it red, but let's call it green this time."

"I think we called it green last time. For two bits, I'd cull that sow and never look back!"

"Are you kids getting along in there? It doesn't sound like it."

"Yes, Mama, we are."

"I think you should pick up and both of you go outside."

"But we haven't even got them worked yet!"

"Pick up your things and go outside, and this time don't leave any marbles on the floor."

" Yes, Mama."

"It's your *fault*."

"NOW!"

"Yes. Mama."

"It's getting close to time for the stage. Pick up all the blocks and marbles and then go get the mail."

And up the hill, past the hog pasture, by the cut bank above the creek, through the swale that during thaws and big rains ran water over the road, we would hurry to the mailbox alongside the county road at the end of our lane. We couldn't tell time. Sometimes, I believe, that in order to either get us out of the house, or to defuse squabbles between us, we were purposely sent early. That was fine with us. It gave more time to build anticipation and reduced the chance of missing any of the daily drama.

Three miles away, down the creek, just above where Hay Coulee crossed under the road on a rickety wooden bridge with no side rails, we could get our first glimpse of a vehicle coming up the road towards our outfit. Of course, any car passing by on the county road was a reportable event. We knew probably nine out of ten vehicles that went by and would relate the information: "Jim and Mary went down by this morning."

"I'll bet they're going to Miles. Mary's mother's had a cold. Probably going to see her."

On occasions when a vehicle went by that we did not recognize, there would be a coordinated attempt to solve the mystery. "A stranger went by in a blue car," we'd report.

"Egans have a blue car. Was it them?"

"No," we'd reply. "This was really blue. And cleaner than Egans'. And it had more numbers on the license plate. I think it was from Billings."

Evidence such as age and sex of occupants, driving speed, direction of travel and any other clues were evaluated, judged and discussed. *"Well, if it was going up the creek, it couldn't be Philbricks' company from Livingston. They were due today but aren't supposed to go back until Tuesday. Besides, I'd think they'd drive down the river and up the Rosebud and not come by the battlefield and Lame Deer."* It might even take a telephone call or two on the battery-powered oak phone with the ringer on the right side and the receiver on the left, but the mystery would usually be solved.

Occasionally a Cheyenne Indian family would slowly go by, the iron tires of their wagon crunching and screeching on the thin, flinty layer of chert-and-clinker gravel. We would studiously ignore them, and they us. There was, by mutual agreement, no eye contact made. Members of both cultures knew it was discourteous and an invasion of privacy to be caught looking at one another. Once, however, a toddler whose face was as round and brown as a cookie, with a pair of great sparkling raisins for eyes, both smiled and waved as we watched with peripheral vision. Although tempted, we did not wave back.

On very rare occasions, an out-of-state car would go by. This was an even bigger, and more treasured, event than seeing a semi rig, which we called a "one-car train." Wyoming vehicles (we knew them by their bucking horse license plates) were observed often enough that there was no electric thrill at seeing them. A real foreign plate caused us to positively overflow with hope and regret. Actually, hope is inadequate in explaining our desire. We fervently wished the driver would stop, perhaps to ask directions. "Yes, sir, you just stay right on this road, and Lennons are just before you get to the Reservation line." Or even better, "No, sir, you missed it. You gotta turn around— you can use our lane if you want—and go back down past both Parkins' places and turn up Greenleaf . . . You're more than welcome. Glad to be a help . . . That's right. We live over there in those two houses. Yes, sir, one is kinda outa sight, but you can see the roof through the trees." Or best of all, we prayed that just once we could be horseback when that rare out-of-state car went by. Even if we were riding bareback, it would be alright. We attempted to train our kid horses to rear on their hind feet and paw the air on the possibility that we could really show off for some tourists. Our reluctant mounts would only respond by slowly backing up, or balking stupidly, neither of which was much of a spectator sport. Although it never happened, we would have probably have been satisfied to give a nonchalant, two-fingered wave—originating at the hat brim—if the coveted tourist car came by while we were mounted bareback beside the road.

Sometimes, if it was completely still, we could hear Emmett's pickup winding up after having stopped at the McCuistion place. He didn't get much of a run between there and Hollys', sometimes not even raising a decent dust. But once he got rolling on the Miller Flat headed for old George Wood's place, if it was dry (which was usually the case) he would kick up a pretty fair rooster tail of red scoria dust. After George's he would drop out of sight. Once he cleared the iron-railed bridge on the curve that the Crow Indians missed, diving their "air-cooled Franklin" nose-down into the bottom mud of the Rosebud, we could hear him upshifting, and we were next!

Emmett Boslaugh, the stage driver, must have loved us kids as much as we loved him. He was Mr. Excitement in our lives. We were his best fans. We never told on Emmett. The older kids knew, but they must have never given him away either. If there was an adult, especially a parent, within sight at the mailbox, Emmett would slowly and sedately roll to a stop, hand the mail sack (our mail did, and still does, come in a sack provided by the box holder, and Lord help the postal official that tries to take our sacks away from us!) to the adult-in-charge and visit a bit—usually about the weather—then on to the next stop. If only kids were in view, however, he would go into his act. He'd downshift, punch the throttle to the floor, siwash the steering wheel from side to side in a barely controlled gravel-throwing slalom, let out a banshee scream, and, as he streaked by, eyes glazed like a man possessed, he'd hook-shot the sack, with the mail in it, over the top of his black Ford pickup into the ditch. We'd laugh and wave and applaud. If the mail got crumpled or muddy, we took the blame. Doing otherwise might get Emmett "in trouble" and he would lose his job, leaving a serious vacuum in our need for external entertainment.

No, we never told on Emmett. But if "all the world's a stage," as Wild Will Shakespeare claimed, he must have known old Emmett and recognized that his stage and his theatrical act were all the drama and comedy we kids on the Rosebud asked for.

COMMERCE

B. Gross would come clattering down the cedar post-and-barbwire-fenced lane from the county road about four times a year. Although the adults tried to convince us that the driver of the asthmatically wheezing International pickup was not named "B. Gross," we were not fooled. Carol and I could read. It said it right there on each door "B. Gross. Dealer In Metals—Hides—Furs. Sheridan Wyoming" in three hand-printed lines. His name was B. Gross. We cared not a bit when the adults told us that he just worked for someone who owned a junkyard that was named B. Gross. The old Scottish chore and handyman Wilkie called him "the Dane." It didn't matter. Thinking back, I don't even think he was a Dane. It also didn't matter that the adults made fun of Mr. Gross's name. "It's okay to be gross," they'd say, "but you don't have to advertise it!"

Mr. Gross's International contained a whole world of excitement for us. It piqued our senses. It reeked of putrefying hides and pelts punctuated with a nose-clearing sulfurous stench from the seeping automotive batteries. We touched each pelt as he named them for us: fox, coyote, beaver, muskrat—once even a mink. The ruptured copper and tin pots and kettles and the car radiators, drooling like cows with bones in their throats, filled the air with a delicious cacophony as he swore and sorted through his loot for examples to show us what he was seeking. He would rummage through the jockey box for a piece of hard candy for each of us. The candy tasted worse than the worst watermelon-flavored Christmas candy we had ever endured, passed out by a poorly disguised neighbor "Santy Claus" after the local country school Christmas program. It was not in a proper brown paper candy bag. It just jostled around amid the rolls of friction tape and mouse poop, and so was encased in a linty pelt of its own. We would solemnly and politely rub off the worst of the accumulated fuzzy filth and plop it into our mouths and suffer the chilblain pain of our protesting salivary glands.

We sold him beef hides. After each butchering, while the cowboys were cutting and sacking the beef in seamless Beemis alfalfa seed sacks and burying them deep in the sawdust of the ice house, we would salt down the flesh side of the hides using coarse ground stock salt. After most of the moisture was sweated out, we would carefully fold the hide starting at the outside edge, leaving the brand on the outside of the bundle. Then we'd wait.

Our avaricious natures were not, however, confined to the purveying of beef hides. We gathered long-necked brown beer bottles from the county road borrow pits. After a dance at the Lee Community Hall, we would drag my partner and cousin Carol's red wagon down the road for a beer-bottle bonanza. Our disgust for drinkers who routinely smashed their bottles was probably engendered more by greed than any thought of conservation, although due to our Scottish upbringing—and those hard financial times—the idea of wasting something of value offended us. Some hired hand was entrusted with the delivery of our hoard of bottles when going to a local country saloon, or "to town for supplies"—which was a code phrase for a periodic drinking spree. While our delivery was being made, we sweated it out. But no matter how long or hard the "toot" that our agent was on, we always got our money upon the partier's return. It was a mystery to us why the beautiful green wine bottles were worthless. We imagined that since most of them had a kick-up poking into the bottom, they were viewed with suspicion because, although the conical indentation was aesthetically pleasing, it did reduce the volume and therefore cheated the customer. We also learned, via the kid grapevine, that certain individuals in the neighborhood would pay good hard cash for sound, clean whiskey bottles. We were prevented by our parents from dealing with these buyers because they would fill them with "white lightning"—which we longed to see in a bottle.

In addition to our beer-bottle business, I learned and earned from Mr. Stewart, who bought both cattle and alfalfa seed from our outfit. The first time I met him I was with my dad while he was patching the meadow fence across the road from the "cemetery pasture" where we wintered the bulls. My dad introduced us. I, either shyly or laconically, must have offered a weak, limp-fish handshake. Mr. Stewart nearly jerked my arm out if its socket and said, "When you shake hands with a man, look him in the eye and *grip* or you'll never amount to anything." My dad assured me later that Mr. Stewart was joking, but I knew better. Another time, when we were shipping steers at the railroad stockyards, I was delegated to count them on and off the scale and to *holler* the count each time to my dad and Mr. Stewart, who were reading and recording the weights and tally numbers. One batch of steers milled and then hit the scale in a wadded clot that made it impossible for a person three and a half feet tall to count. After shutting the gate behind them, I climbed up on the scale gate to get my count. Mr. Stewart saw me there, removed his pipe from his mouth and exclaimed to my father in a slow, Scottish-burred cadence, "Don, if I weigh that laddie of yours one more time I'm gonna take him home with me and the first thing I'll teach him, after he learns to stay the hell off the scale, is to *count!*"

I doubt if Mr. Stewart would have approved, despite his ever-present briar pipe, but both Carol and I were fascinated with smoking. Our fathers and all the hired hands smoked Bull Durham roll-yer-owns, except when in town or in polite company, when they would upgrade to tailor-mades. For some reason, most of the men preferred mealy brown wheat papers in which to roll their Durham. They threw the orange-packaged white papers away. But they were good enough for us. We would scavenge around for used stick matches and artfully roll them in the discarded Riz La white papers with just the burnt part of the match sticking out. These we would "smoke" until they were all slobbered up, at which time we'd shake another match "makin's" out of our Durham sack and roll another. We collected Bull Durham sacks. Not for any logical reason. We just collected them. Once while the men were threshing alfalfa seed, I sacked up about twenty Durham sacks of my own. They looked a lot like the seamless sacks in miniature, I thought. Plump with seed, I took them home and stacked them on the piano in an interlocked pile just like the men stacked the hundred-and-fifty-pound sacks of seed. Mr. Stewart came to buy the seed and stayed for supper. When my bedtime came, considering the disposition of our guest, I went directly to bed— after saying good night to Mr. Stewart and shaking his hand with a firm grip while looking him directly, deeply and sincerely in the eye. The next morning my Durham sacks of seed were gone and there were two silver dollars on the top of the piano. I decided, then, that Mr. Stewart was a *very good* and *kindly* man.

While my alfalfa seed bonanza was a real financial coup, B. Gross was more important as a teacher in the art of barter, bargaining and negotiation. We butchered—along with some hogs and a batch of chickens, geese and turkeys—a beef every couple of months. There were a lot of eager eaters on our outfit and I believe that the beeves were, by today's standards at least, rather small. They must have been young, because the choice sweetbreads had not shriveled away to hard nubbins, as they do in an older animal. We accumulated quite a batch of hides. And just as we kids were about to decide that B. Gross's International pickup was never coming to our place again, he would come reeking, rattling and wheezing down the hill and shudder to a stop in front of the salt house, where the hides were kept. "You keeds got de copper pans, you know, and pots? You got de radiators?"

"Naw," we'd say offhandedly because, unlike Mr. Stewart, B. Gross didn't stress, or even care about, fancy, proper talk.

"You keeds got de battery den?"

"Naw," we'd say.

"Too sumbeech bad," he'd say. "They be beeg moneys now. You keeds maybe steal your mamma copper pots for de beeg moneys."

"Naw."

"You got de coyote, de mushrat then?"

"No. We jist got hides is all," we'd say.

"Aw keeds, keeds," he'd say, "hides be real sumbeech hard to sell. Not worth me hardly haul away. I just come back when de hides dey be worth someteeng. You want candy anyway?"

"You won't buy our hides at all?" we'd pout, hoping that we weren't about to die from mouse poop poisoning.

"Well, you be such good keeds I give you just leettle someteeng for them. Okay? Just maybe feefty cent. Or you wait. Next time maybe dey be better, but feefty cent now be more than I should be geeve you." We, sure that the hide market was on its final downwardly dying spiral—or worse, that B. Gross would never trouble to come back— would sell.

I vividly remember *getting* the money. I have no recollection of *spending* it. So what did we do with the income? Probably saved it. That would jibe with the near-genetic Scottish belief in thrift. B. Gross just quit showing up. My dad took me to Mr. Stewart's funeral. If I saved my share of the hide, bottle and the alfalfa seed money, I'm sure Mr. Stewart was proud of me.

TEACHER

I met her for the first time the summer before I started first grade. Vieno Eastman made the formal introduction: "Wallace, this is Mrs. Bills. She is going to be your teacher." We solemnly eyed each other and formally shook hands, mine lost in the huge, red, rough-knuckled, calloused grasp of hers. Our eyes met through her severe, wire-framed, greatly magnifying spectacles. I felt like the girl in the story that takes cookies to her grandmother on the other side of a great dark wood: "What great hands you have, teacher!" *"The better to spank you with, my child."* "But teacher, what great eyes you have!" *"The better to see your every fault and flaw!"*

It was probably because she was so physically intimidating that I quickly decided I had better be a paragon of good deportment. Due to my genetics (after all, I was John McKay's grandson) and my "youngest child—only son" disposition, this was not an easily accomplished goal. Perhaps it was due more to my being an eager student than any major change in my conduct, but Mrs. Bills and I got along famously. I was even called "teacher's pet" by my contemporaries. This bothered me not in the least. I reveled in the aura of approval. This is not to say that my first year in school was completely devoid of conflicts and problems.

The first problem I had was the discovery that, almost without exception, my peers could write their names, while I could not. Although it seemed to me blatantly unfair, the other kids' parents had given them a jump start. I, in a throat-constricting panic, crammed to catch up. But I did have some advantages. There were several repeated letters in my name. The "W" of my first name turned upside down became the "M" of my second. Further, I loved the complicated, sinuously flowing "R," partially because none of my classmates had two capital letters in either of their names. The duplication of letters did manage to cause me extreme embarrassment the first time I wrote my name on the blackboard, however. The occasion was the exchange of Valentine's Day cards. We wrote our names on the board so the other kids could copy them on the envelopes, which were all put in the top-slotted, red-and-white-crepe-paper-decorated box. Somehow it was probably fitting that all of the crudely colored cards I received on Valentine's Day featured not only false expressions of love, but a carefully lettered "Wallace McRace," just as I had written it.

Beyond writing, there was keen competition to get a star by our names as a reward for a perfect oral reading. The fiery little redheaded Nancy Stretton and I were locked in a dead heat for the championship until one fateful day when I ran into a problem in a sentence that said something like, "Early in the morning I waked to find the sun already shining."

"Waked?" I had never heard the word. I knew that some words were not pronounced as they were spelled, so I finally guessed, "woke." No star for me. The smart aleck Nancy led the derisive laughter as I remained one star behind her on the chart. To this day, I still believe that had it been her misfortune to strike the word, she would have mispronounced it as well. There was no satisfaction in the fact that she was then referred to as the "teacher's pet," although I still believed, secretly, that I had not been displaced from Mrs. Bills' favor. And I still believe that *waked* is a silly word that should never be used in either conversation or writing.

We ranch-raised children rode to school in what was euphemistically called a school bus. In reality, it was a black half-ton Chevy delivery van equipped with a pair of pastel pink-and-white cotton-blanket-covered two-by-twelve-inch plank benches that were bolted to each side of the interior of the back of the panel truck. The two rear doors did not close together tightly. In fact, there was such a gap between them that you could watch the road fly by on rainy days. When it was dry, which was usually the case, you couldn't see anything because of the clouds of red scoria dust that billowed in through that space between the doors.

There was a definite pecking order in the seating. The oldest student rode shotgun, and moving back along each bench, the riders became progressively (or regressively) younger and smaller. Dallas Parkins, whose parents drove the bus, and I were the only first graders, so we rode clear in the back in the dustiest place. "Put your foot in the crack," the older kids would order, as if that would do any good. Needless to say, when we arrived at school, the first thing we did after disembarking was to attempt to shake the dust from ourselves like a horse that has just rolled after a hard ride. We were not anything like the cute, fresh-faced schoolchildren in our books. We more closely resembled the sooty-faced child miners before laws prohibiting their labor were passed and enforced. In fact, although we went to school in a coal-mining camp, the miners' children were much closer to the idealized Norman Rockwellian schoolchildren than we were.

Nancy Stretton's father was a boss at the top of the management ladder. He worked directly under Mr. Foley, who lived Back East somewhere, and, since the mine was nonunion, Mr. Stretton had absolute and complete local control over the lives of all the miners in camp and their families. You didn't mess with Mr. Stretton, or his red-headed daughter. Since I had grown up in a more egalitarian society, I had no inkling of the Strettons' social stature in the mining community.

Nancy's parents dressed her for school befitting her lofty position. One day, attired as usual in a frilly white blouse and a rich tartan woolen skirt, she was ahead of me on the playground slide during afternoon recess. Country kids were always at an advantage on the slide because we brought our noon meal from home in black-and-dark-green-steel lunch boxes. Our sandwiches were done up in waxed paper bread-loaf wrappers that were perfect for sitting on for a slick, speedy ride that the town kids could only envy—or trade for.

Nancy's wool skirt, although fashionable, was no match for my waxed-paper-seated Levi's overalls. My muddy brogans caught her about the belt line, accelerating her as if she had kicked in an afterburner. She had no time to adjust to the shift in speed and, as a consequence, sprawled in the muddy pool at the bottom and would have probably skipped like a spun flat rock across its surface had it not been for me landing on top of her. She breached like a great red-headed whale, called me a "snot-picking farmer" and punched me square in my widow's peak. Without a moment's hesitation I counterpunched her back—right between the eyes. Water, mud and (yes, even though it was unpicked) snot mixed with blood flew from her shocked face. "I'm gonna tell Mrs. Bills. You're in trouble now!" Nancy reported through sobs.

I *was* in trouble. What neither Nancy nor I realized was that our confrontation also might mean trouble for Mrs. Bills, because her husband, Maynard, worked at the mine for Foley Brothers, Inc. My sentence incurred not only a public denunciation in front of the classmates, who viewed me with a mix of awe and genuine concern (one of the less worldly even warned me that my father, a rancher, would be fired) and a solemn promise that I would report the incident to my parents, which meant a serious spanking for sure. I was also instructed to report back to Mrs. Bills the nature of my parents' reaction. Mr. Stretton either never learned of my transgression or felt that Mrs. Bills handled the situation well, because Maynard kept his job.

The plea "she hit me first" did not have much going for it when I reported the fracas to my parents, but it was my only defense. Needless to say, my rationalization had a minimal effect at home. The counterargument "but you don't hit girls" eclipsed even my older sisters' claims that "she had it coming, probably" and did little to mitigate my corporal punishment. In the final analysis, everyone won, I guess. But for weeks my ranch-raised classmate Dallas Parkins was my only friend.

★ ★ ★

Although there were constant differences of opinion and even open physical strife, my classmates and I shared a common hatred and revulsion for the "Japs-'n'-Germans." "Japs-'n'-Germans" was like the southern "Damn Yankees" or the worse western "Dirty Indians," which was perfectly acceptable in that racist era. Our vitriolic loathing and paranoia was not only accepted but encouraged all during the Second World War.

Hatred of the enemy was only one manifestation of our reaction to the war. What today would represent thousands of dollars worth of metallic antiques was feverishly donated to scrap drives. I recall giving up some beloved small animals, horses included, from a miniature farm set, to a rubber drive. We saved great balls of tinfoil from gum wrappers and cigarette packages after soaking and peeling to separate the foil from the paper, and dutifully turned them in to the authorities. Each week at school, we were shamed into competitive frenzies to purchase stamps that were pasted into booklets that, when full, were traded in for war bonds. They cost $18.50 and upon maturity were worth $25. But they were not remotely considered a financial investment. It was the patriotic thing to do. It would help the G.I.s and would help win the war. A

"C" ration sticker on the windshield of the family car entitled us to get three gallons of gasoline per week. Sugar, tires and a multitude of other necessities were severely rationed. Hoarders were publicly exposed and denounced. We quoted slogans: "To save tires and gasoline, drive 35 [mph]," "Is this trip really necessary?" and "Loose lips sink ships." We sang "Rosie the Riveter," "Coming in on a Wing and a Prayer" and "Praise the Lord and Pass the Ammunition."

Our Christmas program that year had nothing to do with Christmas. There was no Christ in the school program. No mangers. No wise men. No Joseph or Mary. There also was no Santa Claus. Mrs. Bills' classes—the first and second grades—for our part of the program performed a patriotic salute to the armed forces. We were costumed in either red, white and blue or home-sewn military attire. The boys were armed with an array of wooden rifles (with affixed bayonets) and swords; the envious girls, including Nancy Stretton, who unsuccessfully lobbied to wear her WAC uniform (see, maybe she wasn't teacher's pet after all), carried a forty-eight-starred Old Glory in each hand, waving them at appropriate times. While Mrs. Bills labored away with her rough hands at the piano, I sang a solo:

> I pledge allegiance to the flag,
> (*the girls raised and waved their flags in semi-unison*)
> The emblem of our land,
> (*flags raised high but still—no waving*)
> To guard and defend our United States,
> (*boys move to front, girls to back*)
> We will all, united, stand.
> (*boys, at attention, present arms*)

. . . and on and on. We were wonderful. There wasn't a dry eye in the house. This beat the hell out of Santy Claus and a manger, any day.

We were warned about Jap-'n'-German incendiary balloons that Tojo, or maybe Hirohito or one of those "buck-toothed yellow runts," wafted into the jet stream. We were shown pieces of the balloons made of surprisingly strong rice paper. There were curious scratchy writings on the paper and smudges from thousands of schoolkids' fingers that had examined the artifact before us. We learned what to do if we saw one of the balloons, and who to report it to. I, and I'm sure others, prayed to God in Heaven each night that I would be blessed by seeing and reporting to the proper authorities one of those "sneaky yellow bastard's" bombs (although I didn't say that, right out, to God) and do my part.

There were armed guards stationed at the entrances to the coal mine. Bud Curran and Hoot Taylor nearly got shot one night when they ran out of gas and walked up to the guard shack without properly alerting the guard or knowing the password. There were prisoners of war quartered at the fairgrounds in the county seat, and local farmers used them for hoeing and harvesting sugar beets and other strategic crops, since so many potential farm workers were G.I.s and unavailable to get the crops out and in.

We kids complained bitterly because certain necessities for our youthful lives, such as candy, metal toys and chewing gum, were no longer available. Probably in order to put things in perspective, Mrs. Bills told us of a letter that her parents, who were farmers at Custer, Montana, received from Moerkerke (Mrs. Bills' family name) relatives in German-occupied Belgium. The letter was mostly upbeat, hardly mentioning the war, which was understandable since it had to pass through German censorship after being mailed. But when Mrs. Bills' parents steamed off the stamp from the old country, in order to save it in a scrapbook, there was a tiny message written on the envelope under the stamp that read, "We are starving." That put an end to our complaints. At least we were not starving.

Later, Mrs. Bills told us about the German prisoners of war

that worked on the Moerkerke farm in Yellowstone County. As part of the contract for their labor, Mrs. Moerkerke fed them the noon meal. It surprised us that Mrs. Bills' mother fed them well until she explained that the work was physically demanding and they were so appreciative. One young German, only seventeen years old, who spoke English, told Mrs. Bills' mother that it was the first time in years they had eaten meat, fresh vegetables and eggs, and the first milk that they had drunk since being drafted into the army. He also said they loved working on the farm and only wished they were home. Mrs. Bills subtly conveyed to us the idea that these German prisoners of war were real people with needs and desires and feelings, just like Americans. How could this be? Why was she telling us this? Weren't her relatives starving because of the Germans? Why would her mother treat subhumans like real people? Was her mother like the suspected Bundestag spy, Cliff Schwenker, who was constantly watched and baited by his patriotic neighbors? Should we report Mrs. Bills, or her mother, to the proper authorities? Maybe, just maybe, Mrs. Bills and her mother were right. Maybe the Germans were not all that different from us. And maybe we learned something as important as reading, addition, and writing.

Mrs. Bills successfully balanced, to a degree at least, the excesses of our Christmas program.

Isabel Bills raised a family and taught elementary school for forty years in Colstrip, Montana. My class was lucky enough to have her as our teacher again in the sixth grade. I'm always surprised and faintly amused when students in other classes of hers infer that they were members of her "favorite class." I'm tactful and tolerant when members of my own class, suffering from faulty memory or delusions of glory, relate that they were Mrs. Bills' favorite student.

FRANK PARKINS

They are all gone now: Wilkie, Carp, Bill Rambow, Walt Evans, Floyd Coates, Elmore. Ivan Seward and Billy Smith are still around somewhere, but they're about as far away from a horse or a cow as you can get, I guess. Even Frank Parkins, who always somehow seemed indestructible, despite his various real and imagined afflictions, is gone.

I can still see him, Frank, in my mind's eye—stirrups let out to the last hole, boot heels down, toes up, Chihuahua spurs chinging, erect as the Eiffel Tower; or standing hipshot, right thumb hooked in his front Levi's pocket, his long back arched like a waterbelly steer calf unsuccessfully trying to pass a kidney stone. Or his badger-gray Charlie Russell hair, straight as a bog-pulling lariat; his striped suit vest with the tally book and the pencil on a string in the breast pocket—I can see him.

The vest was his personal trademark. The Cheyennes had a descriptive name for everyone. A butchering party once came looking for a beef claiming that "The Whiteman With Lots Of Books In His Pocket" had sent them. We knew who had told them that we had a damaged animal they could butcher because it would not make it to market. -

Just like Carp, Frank was a schoolmate of my dad and Uncle Evan, and because of that connection, there was always a job at our outfit when he needed one. He had a homestead on Greenleaf Creek and, later on, some diggings on the Rosebud down by the Braaten and the Brown Crossing. But most of the time that I remember he worked for us.

But not when I first got to know him. He'd leased his Greenleaf Creek homestead to Matt Toohey and was down on the 'Bud and mostly down on his luck, I imagine, since he was driving the school bus that hauled us kids to school. It wasn't really a school bus. It wasn't yellow nor did it have any sign designating it as a bus, but that was okay. Since it was just a dust-sucking black Chevy panel with board benches bolted to the sides, Frank didn't need to act like a real bus driver. So he didn't. He just hauled kids, slowly, carefully, albeit somewhat absentmindedly. The older kids were deputized to enforce some simple rules of conduct so that Frank could drive and dream— which he must have done, because he would often drive right by us waiting at the mailbox in the morning or forget to drop us off in the afternoon. His mind was other places. Probably horseback somewhere. It was the big kids' responsibility to make sure he had his gather before departing the school for the Rosebud.

The alternate driver, Frank's wife, Helen, was another matter. She ruled with an iron gauntlet and drove like Hell was right behind her and gaining on the rare occasions when her services were required by Frank's absence. Our parents didn't approve of Helen, but despite being thrown around in the back of the delivery panel and gathering an even thicker layer of dust than usual, we liked her driving. She brought excitement into our lives. We found the threat of death or maiming somehow thrilling. And the fact that we had a daredevil driver that would pass the other busses satisfied our competitive spirit.

My older sisters and Frank and Helen's son, Billy, were the disciplinarians. Billy's little brother, Dallas, and I were first graders when the bus first ran. While we were at the bottom of the pecking order, we were also protected by our older bus mates. We later inherited other drivers and busses as more routes were added. But as we matured, we could never understand why the young, innocent and weak were not under the protection of the big kids on other bus routes. No son of a bitch better mess with our little kids! Frank's delegating of responsibility by his benevolent disinterest in getting personally involved in the protection of his charges apparently bore long-lasting fruit.

After Frank and Helen were divorced, and Billy and Dallas moved away, Frank worked for us. He usually spent the summers at a line camp on the Cheyenne Reservation at the mouth of Ash Creek on Greenleaf. Wilkie, the boss of the bunkhouse, and Frank never did get along too well, so spring, fall and winter were about all they could stand being together. I don't know why Wilkie and Frank had a conflict, but they did.

My mother also had a problem with Frank. When he wasn't at the line camp, mother would cook for him and Wilkie and, if he wasn't at another camp near Lay Creek, Walt Evans. I think Mother's biggest problem was with Frank's palate. Wilkie ate everything, in large quantities, with great enjoyment. Walt Evans, a small, sensitive, mousy man, was a picky eater; he never complained but just ate a small bit of everything and didn't seem to enjoy any of it. I always thought Walt should have been a store clerk, banker, or accountant, in some profession requiring close attention to detail.

Frank was a hearty eater like Wilkie but he would go on binges. Put a big bowl of mashed potatoes on the table and Frank might load his plate with half of them. Then a few days later he would appear to be potato foundered and wouldn't touch them for a month but would load up on other things. He might binge on vegetables, or meat or bread in unpredictable cycles, but you could count on one thing: he always saved room for dessert. He didn't have just a sweet tooth; he had two jaws full of them! He used a spoon to clean syrup or jam from his plate after eating pancakes or waffles. Honey and biscuits he ate with a fork. But

Mother's biggest gripe was with her homemade fruit, pectin and sugar delicacies that she labored over in a hot summer kitchen and viewed as special treats. Frank referred to them as "sauces" and ate them with a spoon. No matter how much might appear in a bowl or jelly dish, there was never any left over for another meal. "I'll just clean up this sauce for you," Frank would say, as if he was doing the cook a personal favor. It drove my mother wild.

Frank always had an assortment of ailments to complain about. He had a double rupture, but rather than having it repaired, he would gripe about his condition and make an issue of wearing his truss, which was supposed to keep the ruptures in place. The truss must not have worked very well because he was constantly groping at his groin putting things back in place. He also had what he called a "bilious gut" that allowed him to pass gas at some of the most inappropriate times. His bad back was manifested by what Frank called "that damn syatikey." Between his ruptures and "damn syatikey" he wasn't much help handling any jobs that required lifting. He'd attempt to pick up something heavy, then drop it, rub his back, grope at his hernias and "Christ!" he'd say. "That's heavier than a dead priest!" Why a dead priest was any heavier than the unordained living remained a mystery.

I think Frank was in his glory when he was holed up at his line camp on the Reservation. His job was fairly simple. He hauled rock salt in a Jeep Universal to the high points away from the numerous springs and water holes, punched a few cows and calves up into the higher country and scattered bulls, but mostly he was charged with poking around and being seen, in an attempt to deter any opportunistic beef butchers. The Cheyennes butchered as much for sport as for need, and it was a way of declaring ownership of the lands that we leased and a way of registering what they considered valid complaints about the treatment of their ancestors and loss of aboriginal lands.

Being somewhat of a coyote, in that he enjoyed poking around at all hours of the day and night, and possessing a suspicious nature, Frank did his job well. The outfit carried an account at the Lame Deer Trading Company so he could charge groceries and other supplies. Surprisingly, his grocery bill was always reasonable. His only indulgence was the prodigious amount of honey that he consumed. This was not a problem, however, since we had a "bee man" that kept a number of hives on the ranch and paid us with five gallons of honey per year. It was more than even Frank could eat.

Frank was a pretty fair cowboy. He always talked about running wild horses. There were lots of loose horses on the Reservation. Some were broke to lead, some to ride. But some of the owners of the horses just turned them out, and a truly wild herd developed from the mares and studs that either got away or were bred and born in the wild. Frank always wanted to put a gather on the main wild bunch. They were eating quite a bit of grass that we paid to graze, so finally it was decided to try to catch them.

The plan was to ride the high country above Kelly Creek until the wild bunch was spotted, then spread out and prevent them from gaining the high ground. There were enough hands to sweep each divide and creek, forcing the horses lower, out of the timber into open country and hopefully into a wide, roomy fence corner. Carp was the least reliable of the crew, so they put him in charge of the saddle horses. He was to loosely handle the remuda until the wild bunch, under the control of a classy sorrel stud, was forced into the corner. Then Carp would pour the cavvy into the wild bunch. The saddle horses would mix with the wild ones, the fence would be let down and the whole batch would be forced into lower country that was foreign to the wild horses.

Everything was working just as planned. The wild horses were turned back every time the sorrel stud tried to lead them back into the high, timbered country. They were forced into the big open fence corner. But where was Carp with the gentle horse bait? He had lost them. The wild ones milled in a big circle. Every hand had his rope down, hollering and turning them back into the corner. Finally the sorrel stud had had enough. He shut his eyes and dove for an escape. Frank was ready, his lariat tied hard and fast and he had the stud in his sights. Frank ran to fill the hole and the stud ran right in front of Frank's mount, but Frank never threw his loop! They all escaped. The hands rode up to Frank and said in near unison, "Why didn't you rope him!"

Frank looked down and toyed with his once-ready loop. He knew two things: he could have caught the stud, and being tied hard and fast it would probably have been one of the most spectacular wrecks ever seen when the wild stud hit the end of his rope. "Why didn't you take your shot?" echoed in his mind.

"I don't know," Frank mumbled. "Too damn old, I guess." He never promoted gathering the wild bunch again. Tommy Woodenlegs and a few Indian kids whittled away at the wild bunch until they were all gone.

Frank had a propane refrigerator for his perishables and kept a supply of canned goods and "pilot bread"—dry, unleavened, tasteless slabs of saltine cracker–like material that didn't require refrigeration. He was also partial to beans and always had a batch in his shack. He treated his beans like sourdough starter. He never finished the pot, just kept adding water, beans, bacon and pepper sauce to it. My cousin Duke showed up at Frank's camp one time and found Frank, near death, in bed with "the bloody scours and gripping gut pains."

"What have you eaten, Frank?" Duke asked. "Are you poisoned?"

"Beans is all I can hold down."

Duke examined the bean pot on the table and found it bubbling and gurgling like a Yellowstone Park mud spring. "These beans are working," Duke said.

"Think they might be spoilt?" Frank asked.

"You're lucky to be alive."

"If I was real lucky, bad as I feel, I'd be dead," Frank asserted. Even coyotes get sick if they get poison bait.

But despite all of his peculiarities, I liked Frank. And he

liked me. When my folks were away from home and I was in high school, it was my job to cook for Wilkie, Frank and Walt Evans. Walt and I would cook breakfast and supper. All three of them were genuinely interested in what I was studying at school. After supper, Wilkie would retire to his bunkhouse, but Walt and Frank would hang around and visit. Walt would slip into the living room and play the piano for me. Frank would disappear, only to return with his fiddle, and they would entertain while I did the dishes. They never smoked when my folks were home, but they would roll Prince Albert into "wheat papers"—Frank's the size and circumference of a forty penny spike—and play music. Sometimes I would sing with them. I would sweep up the spilled tobacco and swear that our extracurricular activities would remain secret from my parents.

We always worried about Frank when he was alone at his line camp and we would periodically check on him. A person never knew which Frank would be at his camp when we showed up. Usually he was ebullient and full of pent-up conversation. "Har!" he'd laugh, eyes twinkling, "Har!" But occasionally he would grump around answering questions in monosyllables. He might even walk away, put a fist in his back, cock his head off to one side, hang a thumb in his vest pocket and ignore the visitor.

When I got home from the navy, Frank had quit our ranch in a huff, moved away to somewhere out of Billings and married again. I was wrangling the horses alongside the county road one day when about a quarter of a mile away, a dusty pickup slowed and stopped on the road. The driver got out, fiddled around poking just above his groin, arched his back, tipped his head over to one side and stood there. "Har!" Frank said, as I rode up. "Har! How are you, kid?"

"Good, Frank, good. How are you?"

"My damn syatikey is acting up again. Good to see you." He got folded back into his pickup and drove off.

A few years later I read in the *Billings Gazette* that he had died. The paper didn't say the cause. Too damn old, I guess.

CENSUS

I've never lived in town, so I might be wrong, but I've always thought that we rural folks get more unsolicited phone calls than our urban neighbors. I don't believe that city dwellers are called upon to provide directory service, for instance. Doug & Kim McRae live just up the creek two mailboxes from us but are on a different telephone exchange. They are listed under Lame Deer, while we have a Rosebud number. No one knows this, so people find our number and call us and either start a conversation with someone they assume to be them, or ask us if we know their number. My neighbor Bill Allison is on the Ashland exchange, but folks know that we are across-the-fence neighbors, so they call us. Our number is only one digit different from the Longhorn Bar in Rosebud—a six versus a nine—so drunks, and some others who may *not* be drunk—just confused, or suffering from faulty eyesight—call our number. Rita Philbrick often misdials her son, Newell, and gets our number. She asks, "Who is this?

I know Rita's voice, so I reply, "This is Wally, Rita."

"Where's Newell?"

"I don't know."

"Why are you answering his phone?"

"I'm not. You called our number." After this report, Rita recognizes *my* voice, apologizes and we have a delightful visit ending with one or the other saying, "Come visit sometime."

I further believe that people in town don't get calls from house siding, fence post, lightning rod or farm machinery salespersons. Maybe they do. But I bet they don't get constant calls from the septic tank people. How do they know? I don't even want to *think* about our septic tank, let alone talk to some stranger about it.

The very worst, however, are the farm census people. First of all, they send out a questionnaire form. Usually you get the short form. This comes every ten years and only takes an hour or so to fill out. I tolerate them . . . usually. Occasionally we rurals are the recipients of the dreaded LONG FORM. There is no way on God's green earth that one of these can be even *answered.* And forget about being accurate. So the form goes in the "ignore for now file" until maybe six months later when you get the phone call from some civil service person who starts in by asking if you received your farm census form. By this time you have mistakenly assumed that the U. S. Department of Agriculture has decided they can continue to function without you putting in your input. They have not forgotten you. Once the nice civil servant, say . . . Mrs. Peterson, from Ohio, has established that you did get the form, she apologizes for calling you and assumes that you have recently "mailed the form in the envelope provided by the USDA." Much as you hate to admit your incompetence, you admit that it is still around somewhere. "I could have another form sent," Mrs. Peterson volunteers.

"How's the weather in Ohio?" you ask.

She is not to be diverted. "Shall I have a replacement form sent?"

"No. I'm not going to fill it out."

"Oh! But you must! The law is very specific. You must file," she says.

"Have you read the small print in the instructions concerning the legal implications of not filing the form, as opposed to falsifying the answers?" I inquire.

"No. But I am sure that the instructions advise you that you must file."

"That is true," I say. "But the fine and the jail term are both more severe if you are untruthful than if you just don't fill the damn thing out. I read the instructions very carefully and since I want the short jail sentence and small fine—being short of both time and money—I can't afford to complete the questionnaire."

"I don't think the instructions say that," Mrs. Peterson asserts.

"Read the damn thing. That's exactly what they say," I fire back.

"If you are afraid of making mistakes, perhaps I could walk you through the paperwork. Do you have the form in front of you?"

"No."

"I can wait until you find it."

"No you can't, unless you want to spend several hours while we go through the entire 'forget about it' file. I think maybe we threw it away. The instructions didn't say we couldn't do that."

"Very well. I'll have another census document mailed to you and will call you after I am sure you have received it. Thank you for your time."

I say, "Don't mention it."

True to her word, Mrs. Peterson arranges to have another packet delivered and calls back. "Did you get the census mailing?" she asks. "Do you have it in front of you?" As before, she is disinclined to visit about the weather or anything else. "Yes, you have it? Well, let us get to work, then. How many acres do you own on your farm?"

"That's a tough one." I say.

"You don't know how many acres you own?"

"Well, yah." I answer, "but I'm in pretty deep to the Federal Land Bank. I think they own the big majority of the outfit.

Maybe you should check with them and see how much is left for me."

"Just tell me the number of deeded acres on your farm." I really don't think it's any of her business but I tell her. "That much!" she exclaims.

"Is that too much? Should I give you another number?"

"No, no, that's fine," she says. "Not counting any state, Forest Service, Bureau of Land Management, Bureau of Indian Affairs, or Native American Tribal leases, how many acres of leased land is in your farm?"

"Does that count the acres in the county road that runs through the Dodd Place?"

"The what?"

"The county road. I think Jack gave an easement rather than fee title for the road and, therefore, he pays taxes on it, and I guess I pay him for that in the lease. Jack and I don't have a written lease so I'm not sure. Let's skip that one. I don't want to offend Jack by prying into the deal he made with the county, so lets just forget that one."

"We can't," she says, "Just give an estimate."

"And go to Leavenworth over it?"

"I can assure you that is not going to happen."

So I guess, twice. First that Jack gave an easement, and then at the number of acres fenced into the county road right-of-way.

The next query is, "Do you lease any land to any other, person, corporation, partnership or entity?"

"Yes."

"How many acres?"

"Well, let's see. We're back to the Jack Dodd deal. We have a use trade. I get a little land that he can't use, with water at the mouth of Lay Creek on it, and Jack gets a pretty fair scope of country farther up the creek where it's dry but fits in with his operation better than ours. So are we talking net acres? If we are, then I don't lease any land from Jack, so we can forget about the county road deal because, if you don't count the water, he gets more land on the lease trade than I do. And maybe you and Jack can figure it out. Have you talked to him?"

"Who?"

"Jack Dodd. He's under Ashland, like Bill Allison and the Amish, but they don't have telephones. Do you need his number?"

"Whose?"

"Jack's."

"No. We'll just forget the lease with him."

"Who?"

"Jack."

"I hope he doesn't have to go to jail. Who'll look after poor Ruthie Mann and his mother if that happens, now that Lyle is dead."

"Who?"

"Lyle Mann, Jack's half-brother, Ruthie's husband. He got his lungs burned working in that shipyard during the Second World War. Cousin Mac was down there one day before Lyle died and Lyle was going on and on about how he hadn't been worth a shit ever since he worked in that shipyard. Ruthie just looked at him the way she does and said, 'Oh, Lyle, you never were worth a shit before that either.' Come to find out he was right."

"Who was right?"

"Well, everybody, I guess. Lyle, Ruthie. I suppose Mac shouldn't have thought it was so damn funny—Lyle never being worth a shit and all—but Lyle was right for sure, and Ruthie didn't miss the mark much either, since he died right after that."

"Could we get back to the form?"

"Sure. Where were we?"

"I believe that we just finished the 'leases to others' portion."

"No, we didn't. What about the Snider lease?"

"Snider?"

"Yah. Jim Snider, although I think he's a corporation because he uses a 'dba.'"

"A what?"

"A dba. I bet you didn't think I knew about dba's did you? But that's the way it is with Jim: 'James Snider, dba Snider Inc.' It stands for 'does business as' but some people just think he's putting on airs, if you know what I mean."

"You lease land from Snider Inc.?"

"No. *To* him. I tried to lease the grass on the Holly place from him one time after he sold his cows, but he was still leasing from Dora Mees, who was a Holly before she got married—this is back before he bought it—and he thought it probably wouldn't suit Dora. He was probably right. I lease that chunk up above the upper meadow, along the county road on the Miller Flat, to Jim.

"Not the county road again!"

"No, this is on the Miller Flat, not Lay Creek or the river."

"That's a relief. How many acres?"

"We don't know. Well, maybe the SCS or somebody knows, but we don't have a written lease, and, besides, it's on a share basis and not a per acre basis, so we don't know, and I don't care. I have to go through the Holly place to get to our Figure Eight meadow, so it just all works out. That way I didn't have to build a bridge, but I did loan him my post pounder to drive the pilings for the abutments, so I guess a little bit of the road is mine, but we never figured it out. I get a one-fourth, or maybe it's a one-third, share of the wheat, or the money that comes off it whenever Jim sells it. That's all I care about. . . . Jeez, it's getting late and we got a long way to go to get through this form.

"Yes, but I think we can finish the rest rather quickly. Don't you?"

"Oh, sure."

"Alright. Let's do 'improvements.' How many occupied dwellings are there on your farm?"

"Two and a half."

"A half?"

"Well, no, now that I think about it, probably less than a

half. Sometimes someone stays in the old help house for a few days, but we use it mostly for storage, so even if someone was in there full time it still wouldn't count as one. Or would it?"

"We'll just say two. Okay?"

"Well, as George Coates would say, 'Hell, you're doing it,' so that's jake with me."

"How many rods of fence are there on your farm."

"Rods? I'm not even sure what a rod is. Seventeen and a half feet? Is that a rod?"

"Would you rather use miles?"

"I guess. My Dad had an uncle named Rod, but I barely remember him. His last name was McRae too. Everyone always thought he was my grandfather John B. McRae's brother. They didn't know that my grandmother, John's wife, Christina's maiden name was McRae as well, only it was spelled differently, but her brother changed the spelling to McRae, just like John's, for some reason, so it's no wonder everyone got confused. We don't like to talk about it, however, since it sounds like some sort if incest or something, so keep it to yourself unless there is a USDA question about it and we have a choice of going to jail and paying the big fine. Let's go with miles. Do you count a mile of boundary fence as one, or a half?"

"A what?"

"An outside boundary fence. Because if we count it and a neighbor counts that same mile too, the USDA is going to really think the country is fenced up and some displaced cowboy working for the Agriculture Department is going to get all teary and write a country western song or a poem about it and we sure as hell don't need another one of those. So I think we should count a mile, or even a rod, of boundary fence as a half mile, or half rod, as the case may be. Right?"

"Whatever you say."

"No. It's your call. I'm just making suggestions, but both of us are going to have to live with the consequences of your decision. You say."

"Let's call it a half."

"But not on division fences. Okay."

She snarls at me, "Just tell me how many miles of fence."

"Now look, Mrs. Peterson, don't get testy with me. I'm doing my best. But I have a couple of other fence questions. Do stack yard fences count? They really don't fence cattle or horses or even box elder bugs *in*, but fence critters *out*—well, not box elder bugs, because you can't even fence them out of occupied dwellings, can you—so they aren't really a division fence between pastures inside the boundary fence are they? But they definitely are fences, so I suppose we ought to count them. Okay? What about wings?"

"Wings?"

"Yes, wings. Before I sold out on the D Six and bought this place, Jack had built a lot of wings, seeing as how those old Hereford cows were so woofy you couldn't get them through a wire gate between pastures, let alone into a corral. Jack built wings all over the outfit."

"Jack Dodd or whatever you call him built these wings?"

"No, no. Jack Higham. I bought the place from his widow, Jessie. They got it from Josh McCuistion back in the fifties. Fifty-seven, I think. I was in high school and it seems like I was a junior at the time. Josh sold his place up at the mouth of the Musselshell before they built Fort Peck Lake, and came down here and bought it for a song when Carpenters lost it in the thirties. Come to think of it, though, Jack Dodd might have built some of those wings. He worked for Higham some. But most of the time he built fence for Jack Higham on the Tongue."

"The tongue?"

"Yah. Tongue River. I don't know, though. If you talk to Jack Dodd, you might ask him if he built any of those wings over this way. I think Nick Golder might have been involved in some of those wings. And Don Snider, for sure. He's Jim, dba Snider Inc.,'s brother. Don worked here for a long time. Pretty fair cowboy and a hell of a hard worker. He almost quit Higham one time, though. You know how Higham was. Hell for hard work and efficiency. Don stayed in the old log bunkhouse—no, not the one we didn't count that we thought might be a half house, but the one just beyond, where the garden used to be, next to Jack and Jessie's house. Anyway, one day Jack leaned a hoe against the south wall of Don's bunkhouse and said, 'I just figured out how we can get the garden weeded without losing any time. You always go to the bunkhouse before meals and sleep there before breakfast, so when you come to our house to eat, just pick up the hoe and weed a row on your way, lean the hoe up on our house and then hoe a row on your way back. You can get six rows weeded every day, and, hell, you probably won't even have to hoe on Sundays.' Don hoed some garden under protest, I guess, but I do know that he built a pile of fence. Are we going to include the wings?"

"No. Let's forget the wings. Are there any livestock on your farm?"

"Yes." And we zip through a whole list of farm animals that I would be hard pressed to identify in a zoo. Ostrich? Llama? Chinchilla? I'm just damn glad I don't have to report how many prairie dogs, weasels, or box elder bugs are hanging around.

"Are there any horses on your farm?"

"Damn right. What d'ya think we use—helicopter, snow-mobiles and those three- and four-wheel drive chainsaws? Of course we have horses. Jeez."

"Now, don't you get testy, Mr. McRae. What kind of horses?"

"Mostly sorrels, but we're getting a few duns and buckskins out of that Bourbon stud, and one gruello, Owl we call him."

"How many are draft horses?"

"I don't think they were ever called 'draft' horses. The cavalry used to buy a lot of remount horses out of Ft. Keough down by Miles City. They drafted people, but not horses, as near as I know. If you mean remount horses, they quit that long before my time."

"Riding horses, then?"

"Well, like Josh McCuistion used to say, 'sometimes they're riding horses, sometimes not, depending on just how forked you are,' and all the hands would laugh. He was quite a card, that Josh. I could tell you stories about him all day, I suppose."

"Saddle horses, then?"

"Well, I haven't ridden bareback since my dad got me an old MacLellan when I was maybe six years old."

"How many?"

"Oh, I think I was six. Maybe seven."

"No. How many horses?"

"Let me see. Eighteen and a half counting the mares, which aren't really saddle horses, they're mostly just sort of rough halter broke."

"A half?"

"Yes. That Bourbon stud that is throwing those good dun colts out of those sorrel mares of mine that I was telling you about? My brother-in-law, Kent Montgomery, and I bought him from Charlie Dunning. We each own a half. But the stud and my mares are at the M Bar right now. Next year I'll have Kent's mares and the stud here. We trade off every other year. Since the mares and the half stud aren't on this outfit now, do we count them? Or does Kent?"

"Let's just call it nineteen."

"It's okay with me, but Kent might not look too kindly on us rustling half of his stud. He's a hell of a horse, but I don't think he should be counted twice. Maybe you better call Kent. I can give you his phone number. He's under Rosebud, too."

★ ★ ★

We had pretty much skipped over the "crop" part of the inventory because the only crop I reported was hay. I wasn't sure how many "pounds" we put up this year, and the bales were pretty weathered and it was hard to tell this year's from five years' ago—and those in-between years—except for the rotted-off strings on some of the older bales. Oh, we did approach the "pounds of alfalfa seed produced during the last growing year," but that created such a problem that Mrs. Peterson got upset again when I asked if that meant "harvested" or "grown." She figured that it meant harvested and I told her that I had no idea since we don't own a combine or threshing machine and ended up baling some pretty fair seed prospects and I didn't have any way to calculate the number of pounds of seed that we had baled. I told her that we would plant some of the alfalfa when we fed the hay, but she didn't want to even think about that.

She wanted to know how much hay we had on hand, since I couldn't tell old from new bales, and I told her "about one third ton per cow." She didn't understand, until I explained that there was no such thing as a normal year, but *on the average* we tried to sneak by with about a third of a ton per cow. So that brought us to the cattle inventory. It started with "How many dairy cows are presently on your farm?"

"Two," I told her, "Maude and Hulda."

"I don't need names."

"Well, milk cows do," I fired back.

"How many dairy cows are currently in production?"

"Hulda's dried up. It's a real relief, though; she'll put long stringy muscles in your forearms, I'll tell you."

"Hulda's dried up. Does that mean Maude is in production at this time?"

"I thought you said names weren't important. Maybe you better write them down."

She rolled right by that bit of bait. "How many pounds of milk did the cow that is milking produce last week?

"Pounds?" Let's see . . . 'a pint's a pound' isn't it? How many pints does a normal milk bucket hold? Two and a half gallons, divided by what? Four? No eight. I think that's right. If we don't count foam and, say, we have a quart of space in between the top of the foam and the top of the bucket . . . so we subtract

eight pounds, plus subtract, oh, maybe a pint? No, two pints
of foam, since Maude's a pretty easy milker and you get quite a
bit of foam, so that's two more pounds off the total. . . . Do we
count what the cats get?"

Mrs. Peterson lets out an audible groan and very sharply
says, "Cats? Cats! There is no category of cats on the form that
I am attempting to fill out for you! What cats?"

"The cats. The barn cats," I patiently and kindly explain.
"The ones that catch the mice and the damn English sparrows
that some Shakespeare lover imported here. The cats that I
feed in the old cast-iron Griswold skillet with the broken-off
handle. Those cats! The question before us is, do I count cat
milk pounds, or just the pounds that I carry to the house?"

Regaining some measure of composure, Mrs. Peterson says,
"All of the milk that you fed to the cats and all of the milk that
you carried to the house. How many pounds?"

"Well on Tuesday that damn blue heeler pup, Lazarus, laid
into the cats when I opened the barn door and in the melee the
cat milk got spilled. And on Friday good old Laz heeled me on
the way to the house and I dumped damn near all the milk on
the sidewalk, so we better not count those pounds that ended
up on the barn floor and the concrete. Maude's teats have been
kind of sore and she kicked at me and put her foot in the bucket
on Monday, I think it was, so, let's see . . . "

"Just count all of the damn milk that the damn cow gave last
week, damn it!"

"Don't swear, Mrs. Peterson, and please quit crying. I'm
trying."

"Mr. McRae, believe me, I have had some dandies on the
phone in this business, but this is by *far* the *most* interesting
conversation that I have ever had. I am beginning to understand
just how difficult it is for people like you to fill out one of these
forms. Nevertheless, I have a job to do and I'm going to report
you as being uncooperative in fulfilling your legal obligations to
the USDA and you will just have to suffer the consequences."

"But we aren't finished with the form yet," I protested, "Let us continue. Wouldn't we both be better off if I just paid the small fine and went to jail for a short time rather than have one or the other have to pay the big penalties. I hate to say this, but I'm sure that some of the answers are false, and you, as an accessory, are just as guilty as I—more so, perhaps, because you are a professional civil service worker while I am merely a rustic rube that is trying to make a living on a so-called 'farm.'"

★　★　★

About two months later, I received a call from Mr. Anthony from North Carolina, I believe. He also wanted to talk to me about the Farm Census and inferred that I had been uncooperative with one of their agents. "You mean Mrs. Peterson?" I asked.

"I don't know any Mrs. Peterson."

"Don't you people have conventions, or Christmas parties where you eat finger food and wear name tags? I'm sure you do. Keep your eye out for the name 'Mrs. Peterson' on one of those nametags. She is a bit high strung, but deep down I'm sure she is really a fine person. You should get to know her. I'm sure you would like her. If you do run into her, give her my best regards. Although we only met over the telephone, we spent quite a bit of time together and got to know each other quite well."

"Mr. McRae, I'm not going to beat around the bush or quibble with you. Are you going to fill out the Farm Census as required by law, or not?"

I tried to explain the small print and the bit about falsification versus failure to comply by filing the report. He said that he would check that and get back to me. I haven't heard from Mrs. Peterson or Mr. Anthony. It's been years, but things are busy in the Department of Agriculture, I guess. Soon there will be so few of us left out here on the farms and ranches that I'm sure they will find the time to contact me again. I can hardly wait.

ALBERT
TALLBULL

Albert's son, Jacob, was a classmate during my senior year in high school. Jacob and a couple of his Indian friends, Lafe Harris and Steven Two Two, decided they would star for three different basketball teams. Having already played for two of the other schools in our district, they climbed onto the yellow bus headed for Colstrip for their senior year. That way they would have three different letter sweaters emblazoned with three different school logos in their wardrobes. Because the newcomers were transfer students, they were prohibited from playing for our team until the second semester. After the Christmas break, I was relegated to ride the bench for the rest of the season. That was okay with me. I was a sorry basketball player, and the introduction of fresh talent considerably raised the quality of our team. Besides, I genuinely liked the new additions, and what the hell, I was a football player.

As soon as Jacob Tallbull was able to begin playing, his father, Albert, and his stepmother, Rilla, started attending our games. I, therefore, developed a nodding acquaintance with the senior Tallbulls. Naturally, there was a bit of a strain in our relationship. After all, this was the fifties, they were old, their son had replaced me as a starter, and they were Indians.

I received an early release from the navy after my father died. I had been away from home for seven years, in college and in the service, and was somewhat surprised at the ebullience with which Albert greeted me when I ran into him at James King's Standard service station, until I realized that he was reflecting the respect that the Cheyennes show for returning military personnel. "*Ho! Sojer boy,*" Albert said, offering a respectfully limp hand for me to shake.

"How's Jacob?" I asked.

"*Oh, you know. Drunk,*" said Albert.

"Where is he?"

"*Over there at the jail,*" Albert said, pointing with his lips.

"That's too bad," I said.

Albert, with an almost imperceptible shake of his head, said, "*No. Jacob's no good.*"

"He was a good basketball player."

Albert now inspected the horizon above the Forestry Building, "*Yes. Two things Jacob's good at: play basketball and drink.*"

After that, we developed a sort of strange but comfortable relationship. I was interested in collecting Cheyenne crafts and artifacts and in understanding the nuances of their culture and religion. My side of the symbiotic equation came in supplying some of the necessities of life—and requirements that Albert had in his religious quests. Albert would drive down and give me an old ceremonial icon. "I thought you needed this," Albert would say, handing me a buffalo hide rattle incised with strange symbols.

"What's this?" I'd ask.

"*It's a rattle.*"

"What's it for?"

"*It's an old rattle that those old guys used to use. There's lots of spirits in it. But we forgot how to use it and those spirits might be mad if we did things wrong, so I thought you should have it.*"

"Is it going to bring me bad luck?" I'd ask.

"*I don't know. Maybe. Do you want it?*"

"Sure. I'll take the chance, but if I break my leg again I'll blame you," I'd joke.

Completely serious, Albert would say, "*I think you'll be okay.*"

Then it was my turn. "Need anything?" I'd ask.

"*I need some spare beef. Maybe liver. Twenty-seven dollars, fill that gas tank, some 650 x 15 tires, two, maybe three, five-gallon cans of gas and seven quarts real heavy oil.*" He'd dictate his shopping list.

"Big trip," I'd say. "Where you going this time?"

"*It's time to go down to that Texas and get the peyote,*" he'd reply—peyote being the mildly hallucinogenic cactus that is a sacrament in the Native American Church.

"Will your list get you there and back?"

"*I will stay with those guys down in that Oklahoma and they will help out,*" he'd confidently, and, to me, mysteriously, reply.

Although we didn't keep track, I'm sure that, value for value, things evened out. Sometimes he would borrow back some of the articles that were traded and I would ask if he needed to keep the item. "*No, it's yours. I'll bring it back,*" he'd usually say. But occasionally he'd reply, "*I better keep this one. I'll get you a better one.*" And maybe he would.

I finally realized that my specifically requesting a certain item was a violation of our tacit agreement. But prior to that understanding I had asked for a pipe. I had in mind a Minnesota pipestone platform, or T-shaped pipe with a squared wooden stem, an admittedly "touristy" item. Long after I had given up on my order, Albert brought me a pipe. I was disappointed that instead of being a platform pipe it was an undecorated "straight" pipe. Years later, someone who knew much more about Indian artifacts than I asked where I had gotten the pipe, after noting with surprise that it had been "smoked." I was amazed to learn that the plain straight pipe was used only in the sun dance and, because this one had been smoked, it had been used during that most sacred of Cheyenne ceremonies.

On another occasion, when the shopping list was quite

short, maybe just some "spare beef" and "a few dollars," I asked, "What's up?"

"*It's for a peyote meeting,*" Albert said.

"Where is it going to be held?"

"*At my place.*"

"Could I come?" I asked, realizing the boldness of my request as soon as it was spoken.

After a long pause, with a whole lot of horizon gazing—to let me know that the question was a violation of both our codes of conduct—Albert asked, "*Would I be welcome in your church?*"

In what we both knew was probably a lie, I said, "Sure."

After another long pause, Albert said, "*It's about dark on Tuesday. You can come.*"

I'm ashamed that my curiosity eclipsed my sense of propriety and I went. I'm still humbled with the degree of respect that I received and wonder if Albert's reception would have been as gracious as mine was, in my church, or if I would have been as forgiving of gross, if unintended, violations of religious piety.

On another occasion, having been presented with a middle-sized request list, I asked, "Where to this time, Albert?"

"*It's a prayer meeting down to Bear Butte,*" he stated, naming the most holy site in the Cheyenne religion.

"What happens there?" I asked.

"*Oh I don't know. We just go down there to that South Dakota, go up on Bear Butte and pray.*"

"Any special reason for this prayer trip?"

"*Oh yah. This is for the sojer boys over at that Vietnam. Lots of Cheyenne boys over there. And then we pray for The People; for the old ones and the sick ones and the little ones . . . and for our good white rancher neighbors that help us when we need it. And like that.*"

I badgered Albert with all sorts of questions about the preparations, the cleansing ceremonies, the fasting and whether they used group or individual prayer while communicating with the spirits.

"*We're all sorta together up there maybe, but we talk to those spirits without speaking. Like we were alone, I guess."*

I knew that I was being rude, but I asked, "Do you think your prayers are ever answered?"

"Oh sure."

"How do you know?"

"One time those spirits talked to me!"

"How did that come about?" I asked.

"Well it was that third day. I was really hot and thirsty but there were big clouds coming up. There was thunder and lightening in those clouds, so I knew that those spirits were up there too. And those clouds came right over us and the thunder was real close. That grass all laid down and pointed at me like it was little ears, so I knew that those spirits were listening and I prayed really hard. And a little hole opened up and just a little bit of sun came down on top of Bear Butte, no place else. And those spirits then they talked to me!"

"Was it in Cheyenne language? What did the voices say?" I asked.

"I don't know. I was sitting beside that Waldo. He smokes them Winston cigarettes and got one of those coughing fits and I never did hear what they say."

To this day, I haven't decided if Albert was telling the truth, or if the story was his subtle way of informing me that my prying questions were offensive and not deserving of a serious answer.

I don't know if it was caused by some of the bad spirits originating from some of the "medicine objects" that I received from Albert, but I managed to regularly break my left leg. Just after I had the second of three horse wrecks in six years, my neighbor Jack Bailey ran into Albert at the "Big Store" in Lame Deer and said, "Albert. What's the news?"

"Oh, I don't know. Wally McRae broke that leg," Albert suggested.

"That's not news. He broke it a couple of years ago," Jack stated.

"*Well I just heard he broke it.*"

"How did it happen?"

"*Well, this horse slipped down and skidded on it and broke it right off, I heard.*"

"No. That was a couple of years ago."

"*Oh yah. I guess he's in that hospital up at Billin's. Somebody saw him up there yesterday.*"

"In Billings?" Jack said. "You sure? He had the last one fixed in Miles City."

"*Yup. He's up there in that Billin's.*"

"I'll be damned. Same horse?" Jack asked.

"*No. This was that other sorrel horse.*"

"Break both bones again?"

"*Yup, both bones in the same leg again, this guy said.*"

"Break it in the same place?" Jack asked, thinking the worst.

"No." Albert said. "*It was about six miles east of there.*" They both had a good laugh.

Funny guy, Albert. I was busy doing something I thought was more important on the day of his funeral, but he probably didn't need my attendance. I used to take some "spare meat" up to Rilla every once in a while until she joined Albert. We'd just sit, drink coffee and mostly think about Albert until it was time for me to go.

ICING

If you didn't grow up in the country before the Rural Electrification Association power lines came swooping through, you probably have a different definition of icing than those of us raised on the ranches in the West.

You might think of a frosting applied to cakes or cookies; a troublesome problem that used to develop in carburetors at around thirty-two degrees Fahrenheit before the days of fuel injection; or a related and dangerous occurrence that takes place on the wings of small aircraft. Our neighbors to the north will launch into a furious description of some sort of activity engaged in on the hockey rink.

Icing was a winter ritual. When I was a kid on the ranch, every outfit required ice for storing meat during the warm seasons, to keep food cool and safe from bacterial invasions in the oak ice boxes, to chill the hand-cranked ice cream for special events like the Fourth of July or Decoration Day, and to provide shards for cooling iced tea for special guests.

The icehouse was made of logs and built into a north-facing bank. Proper icehouses were shaded by deciduous trees during the summer months, and the roof was slanted away from the sun to reduce the effect of solar heating. Inside were wagonloads of sawdust that served as insulation around, under and over the precious ice. A well-insulated, heavy door was the only opening. And Lord help the kid who left the door open. That was a crime at least as serious as neglecting to close the granary door and allowing the chickens, milk cows, or worse—the horses—to get to the grain.

Any body of water would do for the source of the ice. Although it was too far from our ranch to be of any use to us, the best place to get quality ice was the swimming hole at Colstrip. The swimming hole was an abandoned coal mine pit that naturally filled with water from the remaining coal aquifer. The Northwestern Improvement Company owned the town and mines. The company had a huge icehouse that stored beef for the commissary and the mess hall, where the numerous bachelor miners ate. I knew that it was irresponsible, but I had only a minor twinge of guilt when I peed in the water while splashing around in the shallows of the swimming hole during the summer. I rationalized that since the company had planted sunfish in the pond, the fish, frog and turtle poop were more offensive than my liquid contribution. I never revealed this secret, or its excuse, to any of the town kids, however.

On our outfit, the hands iced the convenient Rosebud Creek. Timing was important. Ideally, the creek was frozen over to its maximum thickness. The danger in waiting too long was that a January thaw might wash a layer of sticks, leaves and silt onto the top of the crop, significantly reducing its quality. First, a slot was cut in the ice with a post bar. Next, the wicked-looking cross-handled saws were slipped into the slot and the sawing began. Long parallel strips, about two feet apart, were cut and then huge cubes were chopped off with the post bar. It was a popular prank to catch someone out on a peninsula of ice and have some jokester chop off their platform behind them, dumping them into the frigid creek water.

Sharp-shod teams of draft horses would then drag the

crystal cubes up a ramp into the waiting wagon and then on to the icehouse. It was hard work for both the horses and the men.

As a precaution, more ice was harvested than was expected to be needed for the coming year. "You never know when a bad ice year might come. Why, I remember back in twenty-nine and thirty we damn near ran out, I do," someone would remark. Everyone would nod their heads and silently agree.

The folks on the dude ranches at Birney, along the Tongue River, iced even after the REA power lines came into their country. Birney residents swore that Tongue River ice was far superior to anything that a damn machine could produce for tea or cocktails for the summer guests. We were not purists, however, and were happy to abandon an arduous chore. The laborers on our outfit did not abandon a grain of wry humor, however. In the days when we iced, during bitter winters when the hands would slave away hauling wagonloads of hay and "cotton cake" to starving cattle, some wag was sure to remark, "Yah, she's a tough winter, alright. But it's a hell of a good ice year!"

DIGGING JOE BEELER

One summer while our family was in Great Falls, we went to the Charles M. Russell Museum. A side room in the gallery had a traveling exhibit of contemporary western artist Joe Beeler's work on display. I had no idea who Joe Beeler was, and although his paintings were obviously painted in the Southwest, I overcame my provincialism and immediately connected with his art. In the language of the times—the sixties—I dug him. While lacking the flamboyance and frantic action of some of Russell's more popular works, Beeler's paintings and sculptures were on a par with Charlie's penchant for visual storytelling.

Ruth was not raised in the West, and since our three kids were too young to interpret the stories behind the art, I felt compelled to explain them. After describing what several of the renditions were really about, I noticed that I had attracted quite a cluster of other folks that were interested in what I was describing. I believe they thought I was a part of the exhibit—a sort of cowboy expert hired by the museum to translate into words what the artist was showing. Hell, I was a hero!

One of the paintings was titled *Shade*. It depicted, in shimmering yellows, one of those scorchingly hot Arizona or

New Mexico days and featured a simmering horse in the only shade available to him—a skinny telephone pole. The horse was using every square centimeter of shade available; the pole's shadow ran from his muzzle up his nose, over the poll, between his ears, down the center of his mane and back and over the crease in his rump. Pretty good story, pretty well told. But there was a kicker! Barely discernable, at the very base of the pole, lined up entirely in the shade, was a companion to the horse: a panting jackrabbit. If plastic containers of bottled water had been available at the time, we would have been good candidates for a sale!

The Cosmopolitan Club featured a lonely saloon with a dirt roof parked in the middle of the southwestern desert. There were no other buildings around, and the saloon exhibited no sign of human occupation. By examining the relaxed, hipshot horses tied up to the hitching rail, however, one could deduce the customers in the saloon.

One horse was a scrawny pinto bridled with an insubstantial chunk of rawhide decorated with silver conchos. There was an additional string of rawhide running through the pony's mouth instead of a bit. There was a Navajo blanket thrown over the saddle, obscuring it except for the rawhide stirrup leathers that led your eye to the small, crudely carved wooden stirrups. There might have been an eagle feather tied into the horse's mane; I can't be sure—it was nearly forty years ago.

The next horse was a tall and beautiful golden palomino, sleek and groomed. Not a hair on his body, mane or tail was out of place. He bore a saddle with the wooden tree exposed and a slightly sloped horn as big as a salad plate. There were hand holts cut into the cantle of the saddletree and a fringed serape tied behind. The silver-mounted bit was attached to a tooled headstall just drooling with finely engraved silver. There was an exquisite, tightly braided romal looped over the horn. Delicately border-carved stirrup leathers ran through the bars of the saddletree, supporting long, flashy tapaderos.

Tied beside the palomino was a rangy, sweat-streaked, ugly-headed brown. Neither the high-horned and high-cantled saddle, the bridle, nor the rusty iron bit bore any trace of frivolous decoration. Between the horse and saddle was what appeared to have once been part of a gray army-issue bed blanket. Unlike the horse next to him with the braided riata strapped to the saddle's slick fork, there was a grass rope tied hard and fast to the horn. Except for the rope, the only other accessories were a pair of gouged and scarred bulldog-nosed taps to protect the rider's feet.

The horses represented three very different purposes to their respective riders. The first was for mere transportation. The second, primarily, for show. And the third, a "hoss" for cow work in the cactus and thorn brush of Arizona.

So who were the patrons of the *Cosmopolitan Club*? "A Navajo, a Mexican vaquero and a brush-popping cowboy," I told my attentive audience. I felt like a western Sherlock Holmes.

★ ★ ★

Since Joe Beeler was responsible for making me a brief, instantaneous hero, I began to follow him and his work.

I discovered that he was one of the original western artists who formed the Cowboy Artists of America (CA). As the charter members of the CA either died off or retired from actively producing art, others who met strict qualifications were inducted into the select organization that originated in a saloon in Sedona, Arizona. As I performed poems and served as master of ceremonies at various art events and sales, I learned more and more about Joe Beeler. There were frequent references to Joe's penchant for practical jokes.

Chas Weldon and some other saddle makers organized a sort of roving band of cowboy craftsmen of various talents. They selected certain ranches and arranged to lend help with spring branding. Jack Hash and his son, J. O., were recruited to supply their chuck wagon and roundup camp outfit for the outings. The participants were a varied group, sort of a lower case "cosmopolitan club," I would suggest. Besides the saddle makers—Chas Weldon, Chuck Stormes, Dale Harwood and George Holt—and saddletree maker John Michaud, there were others: Don Hedgpeth—gear trader, writer, poet and cowboy singer; T. D. Kelsey—top-notch sculptor and sometimes painter; Ian Tyson and Mike Beck—singers/songwriters; and just some good top hands, such as Buck Brannaman, Les Best and Doyle Parker. And—much to my surprise—Joe Beeler! I'm not sure why I made the cut. Perhaps Chas was just setting me up in order to get me to host the crew at a branding on our ranch.

Joe, besides entertaining the crew, gave each participant an original sketch. When our ranch hosted the "Beef, Beans and Bullshit" branding, Joe presented me with his original illustration of my poem "Hired Hand" from a Warren Miller–edited cowboy poetry anthology, *Cattle Horses and Grass*.

Joe loves the camaraderie and inspiration gained at roundups and promotes and attends all he can. One of the roundups he told us about was one exclusively for the CA and their faithful sponsors, patrons and collectors. It was held on the Haythorn Ranch outside Arthur, Nebraska. Waldo Haythorn donated the ranch roundup outfit—tents and chuck wagon—and told them where they could camp, far away from any modern or urban distractions. It was a retreat, not a working roundup, but was an opportunity for both the artists and their guests to rough it on a genuine, sure 'nuf ranch. The patrons had the opportunity to watch the artists as they produced their creations.

Joe, ever the practical joker, took advantage of their isolation as a setting for one of his pranks. Nearly all artists have in their studios a collection of Western and Native American trappings they use to insure accuracy in their works. Joe gathered up some of the artifacts from his collection and took them with him to the Haythorn Ranch. He didn't have to wait long for the initiation of his plan. Volunteers were recruited to dig a slit trench for use as a latrine. Knowing that his reputation was suspect, Joe recruited an accomplice that was in the latrine detail. "I gave him one of my best trinkets, a U.S. Cavalry bridle rosette. . . . one with the eagle on it. 'Pretend you found it in the trench. Make a big deal over it. Then when you got them going maybe hit them a little later with the cavalry blouse button, or maybe the emblem off of the harness back strap. Just be sure you don't overdo it,' I told him."

"It couldn't have worked any better," Joe reported. "My agent was a hell of an actor. *'Lookie here what I found!'* the stooge hollered out, *'Wonder if there's any more of this stuff around?'*"

"I'd scattered some minor pieces of tin and iron, an Indian-head penny and a rifle casing or two around before the 'discovery,' and damned if those guys didn't find them all plus an arrowhead and a stone scraper that I hadn't salted the ground with. It was a regular archaeological frenzy. There was an acute shortage of digging tools. Shovels were in short supply, so eating and cooking utensils were pressed into use. Blisters formed on soft hands and there was hardly a spare fingernail left intact. Of course, I told everyone when the gold rush started that Waldo had told me there had been an old cavalry camp there during the Indian Wars. After they swallowed the bait, I was scared to admit the truth. Those volunteer archaeologists summer fallowed about forty acres of Haythorn's grass and I was afraid to report the damage to Waldo. I've never told a soul about this 'til now and I hope you guys can just keep it between us, if you know what I mean."

Of course, we all assured Joe that his secret was safe with us. "I won't breathe a word." I promised.

RED AND
THE INDIAN

Elmer "Red" Kluver was raised over at the head of Punkin Crick. Back before serving in the Rangers in the Second World War, marrying a local rancher's daughter and running the Bean Ranch down below us on the Rosebud, he followed the local rodeo circuit. He contested in all three of the rough-stock events—bareback, saddle bronc and bull riding. He also rode back and forth to rodeos on an Indian motorcycle—with a side car. Knowing Red, I imagine that the commute between rodeos and home was on a close par with riding the rough stock.

Red enlisted in the army at the start of the war. Befitting his background on ranches in Montana, he signed up for the cavalry. He didn't realize that the era of mounted soldiers had passed. He was assigned to a mule pack company. The mules required two basic things in order to be of service in carrying supplies: they had to be broken and gentled, and they had to be shod.

As the raw volunteers were gathered, their past employment was evaluated. "Does anyone have experience from civilian life as a farrier?"

"I've shod some horses," Red volunteered.

The sergeant led him to the blacksmith shop, showed him the nippers, hoof knives, rasps, forge, anvil, pritchels, hammers and tongs, gave him a round bar of cold steel and said, "Make me a mule shoe."

"For which mule and which foot?" Red asked.

"You just passed the first test," the sergeant said. "That big sorrel one with the flaxy mane." He vaguely gestured at a herd of mules standing hipshot in a corral. "Right hind."

An hour and a half later when the sergeant returned, Red was shaded up on the north side of the shop smoking a Camel cigarette. "I don't see a shoe," the sergeant observed, looking around.

"It's on the mule."

"Where's the mule?"

"Back with the others. I put one on the near hind as well. Thought he should be balanced out."

The sergeant caught the mule and, with quite a bit of assistance from Red, examined the shoeing job. "Who helped you get him shod?" the sergeant asked.

"Oh, I guess about a couple of hundred other sonsabitches back in Montana that were a hell of a lot tougher to shoe than that one," Red said, flipping the Camel butt into the forge.

"You are now a shoeing instructor," the sergeant said. "You will teach others how to do what you just did."

"For a while, maybe," Red replied, "but I can shoe at home and I didn't join this man's army to fight mules. I want to go overseas."

Red didn't talk much about his war experiences, but he did show me his uniform once. I was overwhelmed by the medals and campaign ribbons and the master sergeant's patch on the shoulder. I know he didn't spend much time in the war teaching recruits how to shoe mules.

The first time I ever saw Red was some time after the war. I was just a kid. The crew on our ranch had been moving some cattle and we rode into the headquarters to unsaddle. Uncle

Evan had contacted Red to shoe a tough bronc. Red was in the small corral in front of the barn, sitting on the rump of the bay bronc. The horse was sidelined with both left—and both right—feet tied together. There was a hay bale lengthways between the lashed-together shod feet. Red was just finishing a Bull Durham cigarette.

"Got him shod, I see," Evan observed. "Have any trouble with him?

"Not to speak of. He's just soaking a bit and doing some reflective thinking. I'm about to let him up. Nice colt."

And that is just the way Red was.

After Red married Patty Dowlin and moved to the Bean, we neighbored, trading work back and forth. We played cribbage together during the winters, after feeding. Just before Christmas one year, Red drove in with a motorcycle in the back of his pickup. *What the hell is this?* I thought. *This is not typical of the Red Kluver that I know. A motorcycle?*

"It's for the kids' Christmas." Red answered my unasked question. Want you to store it for a while. Wanta surprise them. Maybe I better try it out."

This I gotta see, I thought. We unloaded the bike. He got it started and swooped around the gravel yard circle—ducking, diving, popping wheelies—his Carhartt coat flapping, the brim on his hat pasted back to the crown by the wind. He was a cowboy Knievel served up with giant hotcake freckles on his scarred hands and seamed face.

"I used to travel on one of these back before the war," he explained, as we both caught our breath. "I wonder whatever happened to it. It was gone when I got back." And he described the bike and those earlier times.

"An Indian? With a sidecar! It'd be worth a mint today."

"Was then, to me. My old rodeo partner, Shorty Huffman, didn't share my enthusiasm for it, though. Wouldn't ride with me. Said it was too crowded in the sidecar sharing room with our saddles, riggins, bull ropes, bells, gear bags and bedrolls. But

I really think he didn't approve of my driving. I went to pick him up one time. 'Let's take my dad's pickup,' Shorty suggested. I looked over at the old man in his chair on the house porch. Rocking. Disapproval written all over his face. 'I wouldn't think he would let us take the pickup,' I said."

"No. It's okay with him."

"When we came back from the rodeo a couple of days later, that old man was still rocking in his chair on the porch. Just like we left him. But my motorcycle was jammed under an iron-wheeled hayrack off to the side of the yard. There were crooked skid marks leading from where I had left it parked to the hayrack. Shorty's dad still had that sour disapproving look on his face. Nothing was said. I just wish I could have been there when the old man tried it out."

"Me too," I said, "Me too."

STORYTELLER

For several years toward the end of her life, Mrs. Carpenter couldn't even tell you her name or the names of any of her children. It was a shame that her wonderful historic stories had become locked in her mind and her only conversations were confused ramblings of paranoia concerning recent events and the fear that "the Russian Communists" had somehow taken over the country surrounding the rest home where she spent her final days.

★ ★ ★

My father and Uncle Evan were wonderful storytellers. In fact, our whole area was filled with, what seems to me, a disproportionate share of great raconteurs. I suppose it is possible that, in a time before television, movies and radio, all isolated rural residents entertained with anecdotes, wry characterizations and oral history. Perhaps the rural community in which I grew up was not unique. There is further evidence of the universality of rural storytelling in the discovery that a particularly good true story was often repeated throughout widely separated geographical areas, especially if the major participants in the tales were known to the members of the different communities. I'll give you an example. A couple of years ago, I ran into an old friend of my father's while attending a cowboy poetry gathering in Lewistown, Montana. We reminisced about several of his and my father's cronies. We began swapping old stories. "Did you ever know Barry Roberts?" I asked.

"Oh my, yes," Mr. Matovich said. "I used to ride with him up in the Judith country. Knew him well."

"My dad used to tell a story about him when he was working on the Antler. It was about a talking cat. Ever hear it?" I asked.

"Oh, yes, I've heard it. But go ahead and tell it again," he said.

And I began relating one of my father's favorite stories about Barry Roberts, who was stuck for several months at a camp with only a cat for company in the line shack. A friend of Barry's got to thinking about Barry and, although he knew he was well provisioned with food, thought he might be lacking companionship and could probably stand some company. He made it within a mile or so of the camp when his pickup became stuck in a snowdrift. Since it was a mild winter evening, he decided that he would walk to Barry's camp, visit, eat supper and, after spending the night in the spare bunk, get Barry's help to dig out the pickup the next day. It was getting dark by the time the friend had made his way to his destination, and as he approached the camp, he saw Barry through the window, cooking his supper by the light of a kerosene lamp. Seeing Barry's cat on the inside of the window sill, and being a practical joker, he decided to play a trick on Barry. He lined up with the cat between him and Barry and in his best feline-impersonating voice said, "Just me and you, Barry, all alone." Barry spun around from his stove and looked at the cat for a while, shook his head and went back to cooking. "Just you and me all alone, Barry," the jokester said again. Barry kept his eye on the cat until his potatoes started to burn. "Just me and you, Barry," the friend repeated.

"Yes, and just as soon as I can catch a horse, it's gonna be just you, you son of a bitch," said Barry. Mr. Matovich and I both had a laugh.

"Yes, that Curly Wetzel was quite a joker," Mr. Matovich said.

"I forgot who the friend was," I said.

"It was that dang Curly. But Curly didn't have to line up with the cat. He could throw his voice. He was noted for that."

I was tempted to argue with the old myth contending a person could make it appear that a voice came from a source removed from the speaker. Although it was a good story whenever my father told it, I felt it would be just as good, and more credible, without the "throwing the voice" part. By abandoning the mythical part of the tale, I suddenly realized I had violated part of the charm of oral tradition. I should have told the story *exactly* the way my father told it. Since I didn't believe that anyone could "throw their voice," I departed from its traditional telling. I should have known better.

★   ★   ★

Had it been one of her stories, Mrs. Carpenter would have told it right.

It usually happened on a Sunday afternoon. My father would say, "Let's go down and visit Mrs. Carpenter." I would be coached on proper conduct while visiting in the Carpenters' home. "You can stay outside if you want to, as long as you don't get into anything, but if you stay in the house, you must be quiet and not touch anything. If you have to go to the bathroom, remember to latch the door on the outhouse and remember to use the catalog pages even if there is toilet paper. Okay?" I would agree to all of the covenants of conduct. But go outside? Never. I would risk a burst bladder or bowel in order to hear every word.

Observing cultural courtesy, Mrs. Carpenter would ask, "Can I get you tea?" which, depending on the season, meant either firing up the cast-iron Majestic coal stove or using precious shards of Rosebud Creek ice harvested during the previous winter.

"No, thanks," one of my parents would reply, observing another aspect of country courtesy.

"Cookies, then?" Mrs. Carpenter would offer. "How about you, Wallace; would you like a cookie?" Mrs. Carpenter probably went to her grave either puzzled by my not liking cookies or impressed by my learning proper conduct at such an early age.

I would find my place against the log wall of the house, under the side table in the small living room. My father and sisters would be seated on wooden chairs brought in from the kitchen, and my mother in the place of honor—on the world's most uncomfortable horsehair-stuffed leather armchair. The rest of the Carpenters would find something else to do, because they had heard it all before, many times. And my father would prime the pump by saying, "Mrs. Carpenter, tell us about the time . . ."

She would still the rocking of her wicker chair, put her knitting or fancywork down, look at the calcimined ridge log while collecting her thoughts and the tension built. Then, placing her wire-rimmed glasses atop her gray head and resuming her rocking, she would say, "My stars, I haven't thought of that for years." She would then pause again for what seemed an eternity to a five-year-old boy, and say, "Ah, . . . but my, yes, I remember it well," and she would begin. . . .

BUCKING HORSE SALE

There might be a flaw in my character; or perhaps in my genetic code, but I've never been a fan of the World Famous Miles City Bucking Horse Sale. A few years ago, I was contacted by a couple of television producers who asked me to narrate a documentary they were making on the event. They were surprised at my lack of enthusiasm. I tried to convey to them the reasons for my reluctance. "It's not about bucking horses or cowboying or the West," I protested. "It's more about getting drunk, dissipated and disgusting. It reminds me of the sled dog races held at West Yellowstone, while I was in college. If you admitted to having seen a dog you were required to pay a penalty, such as buying a round of drinks at Doc's Bar. It definitely was not about the dog races." The TV producers sent me their visual recording and the script. The show concentrated primarily on lifestyle and featured the western roots of the event and, for the most part, barely touched on the extracurricular debauchery associated with it. It was excellent, so, despite my misgivings, I agreed to do the narration.

Although I have not attended the Bucking Horse Sale for years, neither have I boycotted the events surrounding it. Once

I was conned into reciting some poems in a city park. My co-entertainers were a group of interminable and inexhaustible clog dancers who managed to wear the audience down to a paltry few before I gained the microphone.

Another time, I was selected by the Miles City Jaycees to be honored by riding down Main Street as the parade marshal. I hauled the steadiest horse in my string, German, most of the way to Miles before blowing a tire on the horse trailer. I changed the tire and later unloaded German in the city park close to the encounter location with the clog dancers, and escorted the parade down the street in the company of Sheriff Tony Harbaugh and U. S. Congressman Pat Williams. It was a fairly typical Bucking Horse Sale day: cold, windy and raw. After a command performance to "talk cowboy" to some eastern dudes and a drink in the Olive Lounge, I loaded German and headed the hell home. The grandstand was beginning to fill for the afternoon performance when I drove by.

On another occasion, Walter Piehl, an extremely innovative bucking horse artist, had a show of his wild and free paintings at the Miles City Art Center. Walter invited my poetic partner Paul Zarzyski and me to share a few of our poems at his opening. We ate lunch with Walter and his son and debated the advisability of joining the milling throngs at the rodeo grounds but finally decided that was not a good idea. "Let's have just one drink at the Bison before we head back to your place," Paul suggested, "It's just not in keeping with the spirit of the day not to."

The downtown sidewalks were all but deserted. "*This is a good sign. The crowd has moved to the fairgrounds,*" we thought, "*We'll just slip in, have one toddy and visit a bit with Rob Bartholomew and then haul for home.*" Although it was Grand Entry time at the Bucking Horse Sale, the Bison was so crowded we could barely get in the door, let alone get a drink or visit with Rob. We didn't have a drink at the Bison but instead stopped at the deserted Longhorn Bar in Rosebud, had one beer with a lonely Gary the bartender, and drove up the creek home.

For Miles City, the Bucking Horse Sale is a sort of Chamber of Commerce (I'm tempted to say "wet") dream. The motels are booked years in advance. The restaurants prosper. The bars experience an annual bonanza. Homeowners make sure their insurance is paid up, rent out their diggings to fans and pay for an out-of-town vacation from the proceeds garnered. The city and the county make a mint from fines levied on overindulgent revelers. The cops and deputies all earn overtime pay. Recognizing the inherent excesses, there have been various restrictions placed on the revelers. Recently, several blocks of Main Street have been fenced off and I.D.s carefully checked to screen out underage drinkers, and the corralled imbibers are somewhat controlled by roving law-enforcement personnel. Prior to that, a city code banning open containers of alcoholic beverages was strictly enforced.

No one in southern Rosebud County enjoys a good time or good conversation more than Irv Alderson. For years, people had been encouraging Irv to go to the Bucking Horse Sale. At their urging, and despite his better judgment, one year he pitched his bedroll in the back of the pickup and headed his Dodge down Tongue River for Milestown on the third Saturday in May. Irv had helped a neighbor brand a few calves in the morning, so, by the time he got washed and loaded up and down the river, the day's festivities had moved from the rodeo grounds to Main Street. His advisors had told him the most likely place to run into all of his compadres was probably not the Range Riders, the Trails End, or the Montana Bar, but the Bison. Irv added a few numbers to the odometer on the Dodge looking for a parking spot and finally found one about a half-mile away, down by the railroad tracks. He worked his way to the Bison's front door and shouldered his way inside. "The cigarette smoke was from the high ceiling to just about the level of my belt buckle," Irv recalled, "But I'd lived all my life in lots of clean air, so I figured what the hell and tried to work my way to the bar. People with bull riders and obscenities printed on their T-shirts kept trodding on my Bluchers without an apology, but I thought a drink might make me more forgiving. I've never been particularly partial towards beer, but that's what everybody was drinking and I finally figured out why. Those overworked bartenders didn't have time to mix a gin and tonic or a tall whisky and water. I finally passed the word and a five-dollar bill up to the bar for a Bud Light, which seemed to be the beverage of choice on that occasion. When I got the beer and my change, I couldn't get the can down to my mouth for a drink, it was so damned crowded. *What the hell do I do now?* I asked myself. Well, the jam of people maneuvered me with my beer in one hand and my change in the other—both held over my head—to the side door of the saloon and onto the street. It was a great relief. As I pocketed my change and raised my can of beer, a deputy strolled up to me with a ticket pad in one hand and a ballpoint pen in the other."

The deputy said, "I'm sorry, sir, but I gotta write you up."

"What the hell for?" I asked. "I haven't even had a drink yet."

"We have an open container ordinance that prohibits drinking outside the bars."

"I haven't had a drink yet."

"Doesn't matter. I gotta write you up and have you wait for a ride to the justice of the peace to pay your fine."

"Who's your boss?" Irv asked.

"The sheriff, Tony Harbaugh."

"And where's Tony?" Irv inquired.

"I think he's down at the justice court. We're booking and fining our offenders down there and the city police are taking theirs to the city court. It's a special arrangement to help out the city cops during the Bucking Horse Sale. The sheriff stays at the J.P.'s to try to keep things under control there."

"Would it interest you to know that Sheriff Tony Harbaugh is a shirt-tail relative of mine and a personal friend?" Irv asked.

"Not really. You'd be surprised how many friends and

relatives Tony has this time of year. But here's your ride. You can take it up with Tony when you get to court."

Arriving at justice court, Irv spied his old pal Tony, the sheriff. He explained the unfairness of the whole deal in great detail, ending his soliloquy with the plea, "Tony, can't you give me a little help on this deal?"

"No problem, Irv, I'll be glad to help out an old pal like you. How about me guaranteeing your check for the fine?"

I probably should have warned Irv, considering my negative experiences associated with the Bucking Horse Sale. The good results of the whole deal, however, are that the fine was relatively reasonable and Irv didn't compromise his reputation as a certified imbiber by actually drinking Bud Light.

COWMAN

You couldn't describe him as a perfectionist in all areas. We once built a doghouse for a mutt of contorted pedigree named "Zip." Maybe we could blame our tools: a dull crosscut saw, a shoeing hammer, some warped rough-cut one-inch boards and some re-straightened nails of various sizes. We did okay with the floor and the sides, but once that part of the construction was completed we tackled the roof. We finally settled on a sort of modified flat, pitched roof that we planned to nail to the irregular-height sides. Since nothing was square, there were big gaps just below the eaves. We thought we could stuff some chunks of rags in the holes in order to keep the weather out. We had plenty of rags. The wife and mother of the construction crew had grudgingly donated an old "car blanket" to serve as a winter bed for the dog. We were pretty proud when the project was finished. The problem was that old Zip wouldn't enter his new diggings. Oh, if we baited him with choice tidbits from the table, he would cautiously sneak into the crude opening, snatch the offered snack, roll over his hocks and dart out to eat the morsel between the clematis vines and the concrete house foundation. My dad and I concluded that some dogs, Zip included, were "outside dogs" and possessed such amazing grit that they didn't need a shelter even in the harshest weather.

★ ★ ★

Our son, Clint, really understands an internal combustion engine and all of the components that constitute vehicles. Unless it is a modern "black box" computer problem, he can diagnose and repair all sorts of machines. I can assure you that Clint didn't get his automotive talent from his paternal grandfather, however. My dad viewed all machines with superstition and fear. He would try to appease the mechanical gods by faithfully anointing various species of the genus "Machinus" with great gobs of Conoco grease and religiously topping off the radiator, battery and oil sump. And if a machine began to sputter, he would run it until it quit, check the various fluid levels and walk home.

But my father did understand livestock. Especially cattle. We would be moseying along, trailing cows and calves to the leases on the Cheyenne Reservation in the spring, and he would ride back to my position in the drags and say, "Come up here." I would follow him up the side of the herd and he would gesture towards a stream of red-and-white cattle and say, "Remember that red-eyed cow?"

"Which one?" I'd ask, knowing that I was about to fail his test.

"That one with the red spot on her front leg. Remember her?"

"Which one?"

"That one right there following the yellow cow with good bull calf."

"I think I remember her," I'd bluff, not even sure which cow he was pointing out. And he would go into a soliloquy concerning some obscure event that happened when the cow was a calf. He would then reminisce about her whole family, including her mother, his speculation on which bull—long since shipped—sired her, her past calves and siblings.

"That cow with the white tuft on top her neck is her sister. Two, no, three years younger," he'd report cautiously, so as to not offend me if I already knew this impossibly obscure information. "I'll ride back to the drags with you," he'd say. "We'll tuck them in on the way back—against the grain. That works best."

He would constantly coach me on position, or the distance that I should keep my horse from the cattle. Usually I was too close. "Back off a bit," he'd say.

It was always a mistake, but sometimes I would argue or plead my case with him. "But you're closer than I am."

"That's because I'm better mounted than you are," he'd explain. "This horse can get back faster than yours," acknowledging that my Buck, Snooper or Whitey was a slow, hard-mouthed, lazy plug of a kid horse. Or if we were corralling a herd and the animals were starting to mill, "Move up. Move up. But not too close. Don't let any calves squirt out," he'd caution.

He would often quote cowboy scripture from the local prophet, Josh McCuistion: "It's a damn poor outfit where everybody rides behind." Or "Cattle are a string. If you try to push a string, it'll get all wadded up. But you can pull a string anywhere." "Let the leaders pull the drags, don't try to mash the drags through 'em." "One man can drive one cow. Two men can drive two cows. Three men can trail two hundred." Or if a couple of riders—usually kids—holding herd were bored with the job and sat visiting, "If you two are going to ride the same horse, you might as well turn one loose and let him graze." "Start a herd by letting the leaders trail out. They're the smoke that draws the fire along. Push on the coals and you're gonna get burned." Of course, some quotes from "The Book of Josh" were not instructive, just entertaining. If a horse would stumble, then get gathered up and run off a bit: "Like Josh says, 'I can forgive a horse for stumbling, but I wish he'd stop apologizing for it.'" Or if a horse would suddenly shy at a shoulder-high ten-ton rock alongside a trail: "Like Josh says, 'You hands go ahead and laugh, but somebody threw a rock at this horse, one time, that looked a whole lot like that one.'" Perhaps the best one was both humorous and a caution. If a roper was having a hard time heeling calves, or if someone let his horse get out of position either working the herd or corralling cattle and caused an embarrassing wreck, someone would recall the quote from Josh: "Fight your horse; that'll help. Seen lotsa fellas do it."

Occasionally my dad would holler at me, in front of other people, for some cattle-handling sin. "Now you stay awake, and turn back for me when I'm cutting something out," he would instruct me loudly from deep in the herd. This was done in the typically oblique way of instructing someone other than the accused. Later, when we were alone, he would bring it up. "You know why I got on you for not figuring out the deal on turning back for me today?" he'd ask.

"I wasn't doing my job?" I'd guess.

"No. You were doing fine," he'd say, "but Carp was so busy admiring his shadow that he wasn't making a hand, so I hollered at you to wake him up. After that he made a hand, for a while. Did you notice?"

"No," I'd say.

"Well, he did. You should pay attention, Boy."

It's unfortunate, I believe, that "Boy" has become a diminishing or pejorative term. When my father used it, "Boy" was a compliment. It meant that I was not only a son of whom he was proud but that I was an apprentice for whom he held high, but attainable, expectations. "Boy" was a good word.

Shortly after I learned to read, my dad gave me a small book with gilt-edged pages. It was titled "Don'ts For Boys." The book's green soft leather cover was torn and many of the pages had come loose from the spine. My grandmother had given it to him. Its well-worn appearance was a result of much use, not abuse or misuse. It was filled with Victorian instructions on etiquette, decorum and manners. He encouraged me to read it and occasionally would either read some of it to me or question me on its contents. He especially liked me to ask questions about some of the rules in the book. It was important not only that I be a "good boy" but that I understand the purpose behind the rules.

My mother and father could have co-authored another book at about that same time. "Don'ts For Young Cowboys" would have been an appropriate title. "Don't tie a horse up to something he can drag," one of them would suggest. A hair-raising, perhaps true, story would follow about some fool who tied his halter rope to a buggy seat and of the crippled horse that resulted from a runaway. "Don't tie your horse up with the bridle reins," was another. "Don't ride between someone else and the herd." "Don't touch the canvas on a wet roundup tent." "Keep your latigo pulled tight through the keeper." "Don't be the first one in line at the chuck wagon." "Don't play with matches in the hayloft." "Don't use a stout rope strap on your saddle." The list was endless, appropriate and interesting. Even more impressive were some of the don'ts that my parents had failed to observe and the consequences, such as the time my dad put the loop of a lariat around his waist and tied the far end to a post. He soon forgot about being picketed, goosed and boogered like the wild horse that he was pretending to be, and had a runaway that resulted in him passing blood for several days. Or the time my mother's sister, Marion, saw a rattlesnake and picked up a big rock with which to dispatch it but failed to notice another snake curled around the rock. Marion rode several miles home with a bridle rein wrapped tightly around her bitten finger—so tightly that there was some consideration given to amputation. I knew there was a lesson there, but I'm still not sure whether it had to do with checking rocks for lurking reptiles or not applying a rein tourniquet too tightly or for too long.

I suppose I learned more about being a good hand before I ever began receiving a formal school education. Schooling interfered with learning to be a cowboy. During branding, gathering, calving and shipping, I was often too busy getting "an education." Only occasionally would my cowboy lessons be resumed.

Once when I was in college, my father came to Bozeman, where I was attending school, and picked me up to go look at some bulls at Monforton's Ranch out in the Gallatin Valley. "What do you think, Boy?" he asked, as we slogged through pens of bulls.

"Number one-oh-four. What about that one?" I'd ask, relieved for the moment from writing down numbers branded into the horns of coming two-year-old Hereford bulls that he had selected for possible purchase.

His mouth would purse into a straight horizontal line as he studied the bull that I had indicated. "Too chuffy," he'd say, using a term that I had never heard before.

"Chuffy?" I'd ask.

"Yah, chuffy. No stretch or scale. Put him out on short grass with a bunch of cows and he'd render down to a little pot-bellied wharf rat. He's fat. Fat's a good color, but that's all. Remember that."

"Chuffy?" "Fat's a good color?" The lessons required some translation but were good advice.

After college, I went into the navy. While I was in the service, my father died. There were so many things that I wished I had learned when I struck out on my own. But some of the things I had learned from my father only required some adaptation in order to be valuable.

One summer, when I was probably ten years old, my dad and I were out riding, checking on the cattle, their water and fences. We were on Lee Coulee, where Peabody Coal Company is mining now, and ran across a bunch of Jim Bailey's yearling heifers mixed in with our cows and calves. We found a hole in the fence on top of a small rise where all of the staples had come out of the cedar post and had let the wires down to the ground.

Dad had some staples in his saddle pocket, but we scoured the ground until we found the four that had come out of the post—no use using new ones when with a little time we could scrounge the used ones. I held the wires in place while dad pounded the staples in with a rock. I'm pretty sure he checked for snakes before picking up his geological hammer.

"Let's see if we can get those heifers back in Bailey's," Dad suggested. "We'll throw them down next to the fence. You can hold the herd and turn back for me. I'll cut the yearlings out real easy and you can hold them sorta loose. Otherwise, they'll be all over the pasture and we'll have to ride it all, later, to get them back in. We can do it. Don't ya think?"

Every fiber in my mind and body screamed, "No!" to his question. "Maybe," I said.

Twenty minutes later my throat was raw with frustration and suppressed tears and he was beginning to holler. "Easy. Easy! The cut is getting away! Come back here and turn that cow back! Spur that horse in the belly and get him to move!"

Although I'm sure it is mentioned in "Don'ts For Boys," I finally screamed back, "I'm doing the best I can. I've got three jobs: hold the herd, turn back, and hold the cut. I can't do it all!"

Then my dad said something that, if it could be phrased in a negative or cautionary way, would fit in the "Don'ts For Young Cowboys" book and be pretty good general advice in life. He said, "Keep moving, Boy. Cows can't count."

WILKIE

The first time I saw Jim Wilkie was during the noon lunch hour at the school while a group of us elementary students were louting around the company mess hall. This tall, gaunt, scarecrow-looking drunk "borrowed" one of my friend's bicycles and, while slaloming down the hill towards the company store, had one of the most spectacular bike wrecks that I have ever been privileged to witness. Luckily, both the bike and rider survived. "That damn Wilkie like to killed himself on that kid's bike," one of the adult witnesses observed.

Wilkie, I thought, *I've heard of him.*

My grandfather John B. McRae went back to Scotland on several occasions to recruit and sponsor various relatives, friends and countrymen to come to America. Wilkie must have been included in one of the last of these trips back to the Old Country. Or perhaps Wilkie's brothers, who were already here, induced him to cross the water and arranged for him to work for my grandfather. Whichever was the case, he was working on our outfit and had gained citizenship during what he called "War One." As it worked out, the end of Wilkie's first period of employment at our place and the beginning of his second were both war related.

He was drafted into the U.S. Army while working on our ranch and spent the First World War as a cook. Between the two wars, he worked at various places. Although I didn't really know him, he was a character, so tales of his exploits would filter back to us occasionally. The adults on the ranch would shake their heads and cluck their tongues over the news that Wilkie's brother, Harry, who was co-owner of the Sawyer & Wilkie General Merchandise Store in Rosebud, had to fire Jim because while on one of his periodic drunks he had dropped coins between the cracks in the board sidewalks and the town's kids had torn them all up to get to the plunder. Another time, according to the local gossip, he was the prime suspect when the deputy sheriff's vehicle was log-chained to a cottonwood tree and left various parts, including most of the rear end, when the lawman took off to pursue a speeder on the Yellowstone Highway.

During the Second World War, the coal mine at Colstrip was judged to be strategically important to the war effort since the Northern Pacific Railroad was hauling so much military equipment to the West Coast and the mine supplied coal for the huge steam locomotives on the whole NP line. Armed guards were hired to protect the mines from sabotage. Wilkie was working at the mine in a strategic job frozen by government rule dictating that he could neither quit nor be fired.

Japan surrendered in August of 1945. The war was over. Everyone celebrated the victory over Japan. It was V-J Day. Wilkie celebrated, as only he could, for another reason at least as important to him as the surrender: his job was no longer frozen. A few days after V-J Day, Wilkie came staggering down the lane from the county road, singing at the top of his lungs and juggling a suitcase, a bedroll and two bottles of Johnnie Walker Red Label. Reeling into the bunkhouse, without a word to anyone, he began to drink himself back to sobriety. As soon as he judged himself relatively sober and able, he went to work. No one hired him. He had come home again, rolled out his canvas-covered bedroll on an empty bed frame, and simply went to work.

And work was one of the three things that he did best, along with drinking and eating. My mother, my aunt Alice, and later my wife, Ruth, vied for the privilege of feeding Wilkie his three squares, or in his case three rectangles, of nourishment a day. For never was there a more appreciative eater. His appetite was a compliment to any cook, although some of his tastes were a bit peculiar. He loved oatmeal but often on Sunday mornings, involved in a flurry of preparations getting organized to get to church, my mother would serve cold cereal. Wilkie loved corn flakes but not combined with sugar, either brown or white— it didn't matter—and heavy cream, as was the case with his mush, but drowned in black, strong, steaming coffee. "It's more efficient that way. It all ends up together anyway," he would laugh.

The hired hands also loved having Wilkie around. He freed them up to do their "real" work because he did the chores. He slopped the hogs; he planted, cultivated, watered from the creek and harvested the garden. He kept the chickens, took care of the two or three milk cows and after each milking, separated the milk. Every morning I would wake to the sound of the DeLavelle cream separator clicking up to speed until the click changed to the ping of the bell, signaling that the machine had achieved sufficient centrifugal speed to sort the light cream from the heavier skim milk, and then the sound of the skim milk, which was fed to the hogs, plunging into the bucket until the tone was changed and muffled by the froth forming on the top of the pail. He fenced, either with the rest of the crew or on his own, driving to his current project in a three-speed Ford tractor that towed a two-wheeled cart made from the frame and back running gear of a retired International pickup. He did not ride horseback nor, except for his tractor, did he drive.

Each Sunday he washed his own clothes. He would load

his Levi's, long johns and blue chambray shirts into a lunging Maytag with a finger-grabbing wringer on top along with more than enough Oxydol laundry soap and, after rinsing, hang them on the wire fence surrounding the main ranch house, even though there was a clothesline only steps away. "Clotheslines are for dainties," he would say. He did not own an iron.

Hired hands might come and go, but from the day he moved in they all lived in "Wilkie's bunkhouse" and were subject to his high standards of conduct and cleanliness. Bosses and kids were banned from the bunkhouse. Just to make sure that there was no doubt as to who was in charge there, Wilkie hung some novelty signs that he had bought on the walls. Since they were the only attempts made for interior decoration, they demanded attention from trespassers in his domain. "The boss isn't always right, but he's always the boss," one read. "Parents should love their children. For others it's optional," another stated. "Lang may your lum reek," said a third, which translated from the Scottish dialect said, "May your chimney smoke for a long time," which had no hidden meaning except for the fact that Scottish should be spoken if the proprietor so desired.

Workers are often known by the products of their labor. Wilkie's fences were an example. "That'll be there when I'm humus," he'd say. And it was true. His posts were set a bit deeper even though he would lament, "They all rot off at the top of the ground no matter how deep you plant them." His barbed wires were stretched—no, tuned—a couple of notes higher than anyone else's. And in this part of the country, a "Wilkie gate" still describes one that is too tight for women, children, or urban people to open and requires strong men to close with a shoulder-bruising bear hug. He was a perfectionist in all his labors, hoeing out garden plants that were a bit out of their rows and trying unsuccessfully to train that "black bitch of a milk cow not to shit in my cowbarn."

My grandfather died a few years before Wilkie came to our place, so he filled that vacancy in my life. I was never recruited, except for wrangling the milk cows, but I helped him in his work and he helped me in mine. He did not criticize but instructed me past my errors by the oblique methods that are so prevalent in the ranch culture that they are part of the code. If I got involved in "kid things" and neglected to have the milk cows wrangled according to his inflexible schedule, he would get them in on his tractor—in third (the highest) gear at full throttle. He kept the tractor tires underinflated in order to make his vehicle ride better and would go crashing around half squatting on the cast-iron foot pegs, violating the rule "not to run the cows," and I would hear the ruckus and be ashamed that I had not done my job. If I forgot to grease the International side-delivery hay rake, he would casually comment that the rake seemed to be squeaking and that the "bearings probably have to be replaced." Oh yes! He taught me to rake hay when I was probably eleven years old. It was quite a project. I greased the whole rake as he pointed out all of the zerks, I checked the water in the radiator and the oil level, and, after several false starts, he persuaded the Ford to get close enough to the overhead tank for me to fill the fuel tank. After about an hour of false approaches, we finally got the rake hooked up to the multi-holed, transverse tractor drawbar. He drove, as I walked, to a large crested wheat meadow between the ranch headquarters and the county road. He raked two outside rounds while I observed. The third, and fourth "backswath" round, I rode on the drawbar, holding onto the fenders behind him as he raked.

Then it was my turn. He stood off to the side while I figured out the combination of clutch and throttle in a series of lurching failures until I was finally underway, with Wilkie puffing alongside me at a fast walk. He had me start and stop repeatedly, coached me on how important it was to make straight windrows and not to miss a wisp of hay and repeated the instructions of engaging the reel gear on the rake and the raising and lowering of the reel by a couple of shoulder-wrenching cranks.

"Don't drink all your water. I'll come get you at noon," he

said. And I was on my own: free to dream, as long as I kept the windrows straight, remembering to throw three swaths in and one out, panicking each time I had to circle back for the backswath, waving proudly at the occupants of cars and pickups driving by on the county road. It was the most exciting, the most boring and the longest half day of my life. He came to get me at noon and, after we had greased and checked everything, started me on my way again after dinner. I finished the meadow late in the afternoon, turned off the tractor, grabbed my nearly empty canvas water sack and walked home. Wilkie went with me to retrieve the rig. He opened the impossible "Wilkie gate," drove through and closed the gate, and I drove triumphantly home. He unhooked the rake and, riding on the drawbar, told me to park the tractor in the open shed beside the blacksmith shop. As we approached the slot in the shed at a goodly clip, he cautioned me to "throttle back." With rising panic at the too-fast-approaching shed, I pulled the throttle all the way "back" and ran clear through the far wall of the shed. When I finally got the whole thing shut down, Wilkie was lying on the ground. "I've killed him!" I thought. No. He was still alive, but rolling around on the ground in gales of laughter.

"I taught you everything you needed to know except how to stop," he said. "Now we'll find some boards and fix the shed and not tell anyone." Until now, neither of us ever mentioned the incident again.

Jim Wilkie did not drink. He just got drunk. Nearly without exception, he planned his drinking bouts so they caused the least disruption in the smooth flow of the ranch. Only once, when the rest of the hands were on the roundup and I was in high school, did he fail to resist temptation and leave me to do all of his chores. I can't say that I wasn't just as disgusted as everyone else on the ranch used to get with him. But it didn't hurt me, after football practice and before the school bus came, to fill in for Jim. After all, he had done the same for all of us for years. But despite his usual thoughtful planning of when he went on his toots, he was an awful drunk. When he was drinking there was a period when he was marvelously entertaining. Beyond that brief interlude he was, however, completely insufferable. I believe that my father was bothered, with the exception of some long-suffering bartenders, more than anyone else by Jim's sprees. Usually Jim would catch a ride to town with the stage driver to start his drinking.

Despite his calling Forsyth a "puky town," it was a good place for him to be on a bender. He would get a room in the Joseph Hotel and do most of his drinking in the Oak Room, where the co-owners, Lou Dalby and Dom DeSocio, would take as good care of Jim as he would allow. Lou and Dom would try to get some food in him, try to keep him from getting in a fight and attempt to get him to his room. After three or four days of debauchery, Jim would catch a ride back to the ranch, his town fedora smashed, ingloriously drunk and with a good supply of tapering-off liquor. "Drink rum and you'll never have a hangover," Wilkie pontificated prior to proving that theory wrong. He would go through various degrees of drunkenness for several days, sometimes sobering up on several cases of beer. During some of his "better times" he would find the determination and coordination to wander to our house, usually in the middle of the night. "Wake up, damn you, Donald McRae," he'd rave at the top of his lungs. "I want to talk to you." They'd sit in the kitchen for hours as Wilkie mumbled or shouted through his rambling monologues. "Are you listenin' to me, Don McRae?" he'd shout. Dad would answer barely loud enough for me to hear as I lay awake in my bed. "Good, then, because I want to sing to you," and Wilkie would give his version of "I Wonder Who's Kissing Her Now," which started out: "I wonder who knocked up our cow. Someone must have done it somehow . . ." After the solo, I might drift off to sleep to be awakened later hearing Wilkie lament, "Oh Don! I'm no damn good. I'm even built upside down! My nose runs and my feet smell! I'm the black sheep of my family. Harry was a good man. Harry was a Mason. Peter was a good man. A businessman. Peter was successful. Peter was a Mason. And what am I? I'm a disgrace to the family. I'm the black sheep. Harry was a good man. Peter was a good man. . . ." on and on his circuitous ramblings would continue. Sometimes I would be awake to hear the conclusion of this particular soliloquy: "I'm just no good. An old worthless drunk. God, man, I'm a bad influence on the family. I'm too old to work. I'm just a burden. I've got veteran benefits. You don't need me. You ought to fire me! Why don't you just fire me, Donald McRae? I'll tell you why. Because you never did hire me! You can't fire me. You didn't hire me. So there, Donald McRae! You're not so damn smart! You can't fire me!"

He was right. No one could fire him. One day he reinforced his no-firing position by telling my father that he was no longer going to take wages. He was serious and sober. Despite my dad's arguing, Wilkie was adamant. He would work for room and board and live off of his Social Security "dole."

He never quit working. He never quit drinking. He died one night in a stupor in his rented room at the Joseph Hotel. We buried him in the veterans' cemetery in Forsyth, even though it is a "puky town." He was a very good man.

CHARLIE

After graduating from college at Montana State, I joined the navy. I had passed a written exam and qualified for Officer Candidate School. I was flown to Seattle to be sworn in. My orders instructed me to report for OCS in Newport, Rhode Island.

When I first met my Pennsylvania-raised wife, Ruth, I asked her if she had ever been "west."

"Yes," she replied, "to Ohio." This struck me as ridiculously humorous. Then, after considering, I realized that I had never been farther east than Greencastle, Indiana, before entering the navy.

My best friend at OCS, Bob Jaffee, wrote a graduation skit about a day in the life of a student at OCS. I memorized my role as the narrator of the show. Part of the lines read, "In the fall of 1958, you left your home in the West and headed for Newport, Rhode Island! The vacation-land of the Vanderbilts! The home of the America's Cup! Newport-by-the-Sea. Even if we tired of the gay and carefree life in the beautiful countryside of rustic old New England, there was always Boston to the north, New York to the south, and nearby, those quaint, mysterious seaside resorts, Providence, Lowell and Fall River!" Although written tongue-in-cheek, for me, there was some truth to it. I was in a new and exciting part of the country.

I was also a naive rural ranch kid who, while not lacking company, was homesick. During the first weekend liberty, I went to a movie, *Big Country*. It was a new, high-budget western starring Charlton Heston as a ranch foreman and Gregory Peck as a ship's captain. They were both vying for the love of the rancher's daughter, Jean Simmons. "Ever seen anything this big?" Charlton taunted Gregory as they looked over the ranch.

"No," the Captain replied. Then after a long pause . . . "unless it would be the sea." I hadn't really seen the sea—yet—so *Big Country* didn't help my homesickness.

In his book *Walden*, Thoreau stated, "I never found the companion that was so companionable as solitude. We are for the most part more lonely when we go abroad among men than when we stay in our chambers." I found that to be true. Most weekends I would rent a bicycle at a shop in Newport and pedal my way north, on a winding road, to a bird sanctuary, where I sought Thoreau's "companionable solitude."

Later, after I was commissioned and assigned to a ship that was based in Little Creek, Virginia, I bought a red MG sports car that was intended to be a "girl getter." The car was a disaster, both mechanically and in attracting female companionship, but it did let me search for, though rarely find, my solitude—in nameless villages along the Chesapeake Bay, the outer sand strip islands of North Carolina, and in Williamsburg, Virginia. I missed the Big Country. I missed the West.

One weekend I drove to Washington, D. C. I visited the Smithsonian and the Washington, Lincoln and Jefferson Memorial monuments. Finally, I drove by the White House, parked and went into the Capitol Building, where I found a companion with which to share my yearning for home—in the basement of the capitol, each state has a statue or two of their favored citizens. I saw him through a maze of marble and bronze figures, many dressed in breeches and frock coats and sporting powdered wigs. His head was tipped off to one side as if he was studying, or judging, a nearly completed oil painting. Was it the huge mural of *Lewis and Clark Meeting The Flathead Indians* in the capitol building in Helena? Or perhaps *When Horses Talk War* . . . or *Laugh Kills Lonesome*. But wait! The painting was without human figures. In it buffalo were streaming water from their coats, having just crossed the Missouri. The herd was being escorted by a detachment of gray wolves. What were those mountains faintly seen through the river mists? The Belts? The Highwoods? That was the painting he was studying, *When the Land Belonged to God*. We could both see it. He had his palette in his left hand, a broad, stiff-bristled brush in his right. I didn't need to read his name, or state, in the raised letters at the base of the bronze. "Howdy, Charlie," I must have said aloud, because people nearby looked at me strangely. I didn't give a damn.

LEE KIMBALL

It was a ritual he observed each morning. Carefully climbing his rickety wooden stepladder, in each classroom he would open the face of the oak-cased pendulum clock, then set and wind it. Fishing the leather-fobbed railroad watch from one of the breast pockets in his overalls, he would compare the two timepieces, ensuring they were keeping identical time. If they were exactly the same, he would then slowly and carefully wind the classroom clock.

The next step was to carefully dust the top of the case and wipe any residual fingerprints from the glass clock face. Unless some more pressing emergency interfered, this was done before classes started. The fact that each clock kept nearly perfect time did not affect the ritual. Occasionally, however, we were released from our usual regimen of learning one of the three R's and were treated to the welcome distraction by the daily clock-winding ceremony.

While attending elementary and high school, we students did not enjoy the benefits of psychologists, nurses or guidance counselors. We didn't need them. We had Mr. Kimball. As was the case with our teachers and the superintendent, all school personnel, with the exception of the bus drivers, had no first names. Their surnames were preceded by Mr., Mrs. or Miss. Although he was the janitor, due to the high measure of respect held for him in the community, Mr. Kimball was extended the same courtesy and deference; his name was not Lee Kimball. It was Mr. Kimball.

Mr. and Mrs. Kimball came to our country in 1909. In 1912, they filed on a "desert claim," making them one of the first in the wave of optimistic homesteaders who followed in the teens and '20s. He was viewed as one of the natural leaders in the klatch of those unfortunate prospective farmers that, for a tragically brief time, filled the West. My father recalled a Fourth of July celebration held at the Castle Rock Community Hall when the designated holiday orator, Mr. Kimball, predicted a rosy future for farming on Emmels Creek, west of Colstrip. Dad remembered suspecting, at the time, that the glowing forecast of green and golden fields, red barns, and stately white-painted farmhouses was probably, and tragically, overly optimistic. My father was correct. With the drought a few years later, the homestead-era optimism died in the dust.

Although he was able to hold onto the land, Mr. Kimball was forced to find other employment. By the time I entered first grade, in 1941, Mr. Kimball was already an institution at the Colstrip School, where he was employed as the janitor.

I initially thought him to be a large and intimidating person. If it had been a word in my limited vocabulary at that time, he would have been an *ogre*. I knew all about the Three Billy Goats Gruff and imagined him to be an evil troll living under a bridge. Under his blue-and-white-striped railroader's cap he had a full head of wild and unkempt gray hair. His protruding lower jaw was filled with sharp canine teeth perfect for chomping on small children like the denizen faced by the little girl with the red hooded cape. I soon learned that his appearance was not a true reflection of his character, however.

He wore the same uniform every day: a blue chambray shirt

buttoned at the collar, a heavy pair of work shoes and clean, pressed, faded blue bib overalls. In each hip pocket he carried another important object: one was a soft white cloth used in wiping away errant spills and fingerprints; the other was a red-and-white bandana, or workman's handkerchief, to wipe a crying child's nose, eyes and upper lip, or with an added spot of saliva, to scrub the playground dirt from a scuffed knee to check the seriousness of the injury and give some measure of comfort to the wounded.

The construction of the new redbrick school, which replaced the two white-painted frame buildings, was completed shortly after Mr. Kimball's wife's death in 1947. The new school included one room in the basement with CUSTODIAN printed in gold letters on the oak door of his apartment. It contained various janitorial supplies, his office and living quarters. Although it was off-limits to students, we knew his tiny Spartan home included a small refrigerator, a narrow iron-framed bed and a hot plate for cooking his meals.

Despite his spare apartment, being forced to leave his farm, his few possessions and assumed low salary, he was perhaps the happiest of persons. His real wealth was in his kindness and love to others. These traits were recognized and reciprocated by the whole community. His main duties consisted of keeping the coal-fired boiler functioning, cleaning, and replacing frequently broken fixtures, desks and windows. These functions, however, were only incidental to his real job.

Elementary school girls were expected to wear rough, thigh-length, tan stockings held in place by a garter belt. This was especially true for my sisters and other female rural students. Although it was a statement of their being from the country and "bus students," the stockings represented not a style but a practical necessity during the colder months of the school year. The ugly stockings insulated country girls' legs on frigid walks to the mailbox or as insurance in the case of the bus breaking down. My sister Marjorie was warned by our mother that if she didn't wear the stockings, she would "catch her death of cold, miss school, and be required to repeat the grade she was currently in." Marjorie was mortified one day when her garter belt failed and one of her stockings kept falling down. Sensing her frustration and seeing her tears, Marjorie's teacher ascertained the cause of her distress and tried, unsuccessfully, to repair the cause of her problem. "Why don't you take off both stockings? You really don't need to wear them today. I'll give you a paper bag to put them in and you can take them home after school. We'll put them in with the garter belt because I can't fix it."

Not to be mollified by this distressing appraisal of her situation, the sobbing Marjorie replied, "Mr. Kimball could fix it."

Mr. Kimball never retired. He died on the job. After his death, as a tribute to his value to the school and community, one graduating senior was recognized for leadership, scholarship and overall contributions to the local common good by being named the recipient of the annual Kimball Award. It was a coveted and fitting recognition of a man who could fix broken windows and desks, wind and check the clocks, settle disputes between friends, mend broken hearts and even mend an occasional broken garter belt for a despondent little girl.

MR. COLBERT

I didn't know Mr. Colbert. He was buried, alongside his wife, in one of the three cemeteries at Ashland long before my time. It isn't necessary to know him, however. All that you have to do is listen to the stories of the old-timers along Tongue River and the Rosebud and you will learn about him. Why are there still Colbert stories floating around? Because he was a wonderfully entertaining character. All of the good local storytellers were adept vocal mimics, and the "Colbert voice" was so distinctive that it begged imitation. He talked in a complete "conehead" monotone, with no inflection in his speech.

"Just how tall *are* you, Mr. Colbert?" the storyteller would recount the question for his audience. *"I-never-can-remember-if-it's-six-foot-seven-or-seven-foot-six . . . ,"* he would reply.

Once, when putting siding on his two-story ranch house on Tongue River, located between the Barringer place and the Cheyenne Reservation, he and his helpers had erected a rickety scaffold to the upper story. When his wife came out to announce that dinner was ready, for the first time, the whole crew moved to the ladder at one end of the scaffold. Slowly, sedately, like the *Titanic* beginning its final dive to the bottom, the temporary skeleton began to collapse. Mr. Colbert informed his wife with considerable presence of mind, *"Prepare-yourself, madam, as-we-are-coming-down . . ."*

Mr. Colbert herded sheep for Freeman Philbrick while putting his stake together in order to acquire a ranch of his own. One year, after bringing in his band of sheep to the headquarters of Freem's E V Ranch for fall weaning, he and the rest of the herders and the crew were invited to eat at the Philbrick table. Freeman's wife, Mary, was not only proper but almost regal in her bearing and demeanor, befitting her New England roots. After the first helping, Mrs. Philbrick graciously inquired, "May I pass you anything, Mr. Colbert?" Acknowledging both the offer and his extreme height and length of arm, Mr. Colbert replied, *"Thank-you, madam, I-believe-that-I-can-reach-everything-from-here . . ."*

Another time, Mary Philbrick was at the mailbox waiting for the stage when she observed a gangly, bony Ichabod Crane look-alike apparition approaching on a jaded, lathered horse. *"Please-inform-Freeman-that-I-just-put-three-steers-in-the-meadow—two-through-the-gate-and-one-through-the-fence . . . ,"* Mr. Colbert reported.

While working for Freem Philbrick, Mr. Colbert, in the usual mode of those hired hands who were putting their stake together, let his wages "ride," or accumulate. The employer might, however, buy requested employee necessities while in town and subtract the cost from the accumulated stake balance. Only necessities were ordered for the employer's infrequent trips to town.

In an uncharacteristic exception to this thrifty practice, Mr. Colbert ordered a new automobile. Frank Levi arranged to deliver the car to the Philbrick ranch, but when he arrived with the new Overland, Mr. Colbert was out with a band of sheep. Frank left the car and caught a ride back to town. Prior to his departure, Frank left the owner's manual and some basic instructions for driving with the Philbricks' cook, Mrs. Price.

Long after all of the visitors and the headquarters crew had thoroughly examined and admired the Overland, and Mrs. Price had forgotten the detailed operating instructions, Mr. Colbert came in with the sheep in his charge. After helping Mrs. Price with the supper dishes, it was time for the proud new owner to learn to drive his prize. Admiring neighbors and the whole ranch crew assembled to observe this historic event. With the operator's book in hand, Mrs. Price along with her pupil, Mr. Colbert, approached the Overland. Mrs. Price began reading aloud about the manually operated windshield wipers, the oil reservoir, how to work the jack and change a tire, as the audience tittered and the owner grew more impatient. Finally, Mrs. Price worked her way to the important parts: how to start and actually drive the car. As she instructed, the spark was advanced, the gas rate to the carburetor was set and the shift levers adjusted, putting the transmission in neutral. Mrs. Price climbed into the passenger seat as Mr. Colbert spun the crank. "Pull the crank out when it starts! the book says."

"*That-I-will-do-if-it-does . . .*"

Finally, with a stammering roar, the engine caught. Mr. Colbert cached the crank and folded his lanky frame into the driver's seat. "Reduce the idle speed by adjusting the fuel lever!" Mrs. Price shouted. Before they actually got moving, Mr. Colbert was streaming sweat and had a great deal of practice in cranking and getting in and out of the car.

"Give it more gas and it won't die when you spur it in the belly to get that critter untracked," some wag advised. The advice was taken and off they went in a lurching, roaring start.

Around and around in dizzying circles they went—dust flying, sheep dogs snapping at the tires, spectators cheering and laughing—until Mr. Colbert, finally understanding that there was a relationship between the steering wheel and the vehicle's direction, turned the wheel and, gaining a small measure of control, went staggering and slaloming up the lane. Mrs. Price kept shouting instructions as she flipped through the pages of Overland scripture. His gaunt jaws clenched, the driver was barely able to maintain a consistent direction, being more used to bridle reins and driving lines than steering wheels, until the distraught Mrs. Price heard a panicked voice inform her, "*You-better-read-another-chapter-Price, we're-a'comin'-to-a-board-gate . . .*"

That is always the end of the story. I don't know what happened to the gate or the car, but I suppose that isn't important.

Eventually Mr. Colbert cashed in his accumulated wages from herding sheep and bought a ranch on the Tongue River. While there, he acquired a balky saddle horse. Someone informed him that Hokey Pokey was a sure-fire cure for a horse that refused to move, so he bought a bottle. Hokey Pokey, or High Life, was a chemical Hot Shot, carbon disulphide. I'm not sure what sort of a reaction took place, but applied to a horse it had the same effect that turpentine has when applied to the nether parts of a dog or cat. One day while riding the horse over east of the river in the foothills of Cook Mountain, the horse just froze up and refused to move. He wouldn't lead and no amount of slapping the reins or spurring produced any movement. Aha! Mr. Colbert remembered that he had his bottle of yet-untested Hokey Pokey in a saddle pocket. Later he told of the results: "*I-took-the-bottle-of-Hokey-Pokey-from-my-saddle-pocket, removed-the-cork, and-placed-three-drops-on-the-root-of-his-tail . . . I-rode-three-jumps-and-walked-six-miles . . .*"

No, I never met Mr. Colbert but I know him from the stories told by Genie May Garfield, her father, Mac Philbrick, Mrs. Carpenter and my dad. The final story of Mr. Colbert is not often told, however. One would assume that he was just another colorful character, but he was more than that. He came to the country in 1884 and became a successful, admired and prosperous rancher. He died a broken, penniless man in the thirties, having lost his money while a director in the Rosebud State Bank, after turning all of his assets over to the bank in an attempt to avoid a run on the bank that would impoverish all of the depositors. He failed and so did the bank.

A TRIO OF CULTURAL EVENTS

Cultural events in southern Rosebud County, Montana, are pretty hard to come by. Sometimes they come in clusters and you have to arrange your schedule carefully so you don't miss the opportunity to experience them. Once I attended three widely different occasions on the same day.

POWWOW

Because roughly half of my high school class were members of the tribe and I acquired not only friends but also an interest in their culture and traditions, I feel an attraction to attend the annual powwow on the Northern Cheyenne Reservation at the Forks of Lame Deer Creek. I suspect that most of the non-Indians that attend are wannabes for a day. They put on silver and turquoise from an Indian culture a thousand miles away, or beadwork, elk teeth and bear claws that somehow look a bit ludicrous on whites. The Cheyennes slyly call them "reverse apples." You know, "red on the inside, white on the outside." I've never been particularly comfortable wearing beadwork. It's like a Kurd in a kilt, a Samoan sporting a babushka or a Norwegian wearing a turban. However, I do have a beaded buckle, snapped on a horsehair belt, that I've been wearing since I received it in a "giveaway" sponsored by the Flatness family at a powwow a couple of years ago. Maybe I'm kidding myself and "wannabe" just a bit pink inside.

The buckle is the only suspect article in my costume, however. The rest is pure cowboy, right down to the Levi's pant legs "shot gunned," or stuffed, into the tall red tops of my Paul Bond boots.

So, anyway, I attend the powwow, seeing and being seen, greeting and being greeted, renewing old acquaintances and making a few new friends. You must realize that an Anglo is never completely comfortable at a powwow. We're sort of like toads at the frog convention. This is only fair, of course. Maybe it's their way of getting even with us. You know, it's the "Custer Died For Your Sins" syndrome. I've come to accept being the last one waited on at the "Genuine Indian Tacos" stand, for instance. I really don't mind. And further, I've never been hassled. But there is, always, that slightly unnerving possibility. In reality you're never really sure that you're not being, if not actually hassled, at least tweaked by subtle Indian humor. For instance, I'm off-handedly introduced to an old-timer, prefaced by the question, "Know who this cowboy is?"

"I don't know," is the answer.

"This is that poet guy, Wally McRae."

After a long pause the gray braid says, simply, "Big Man." And I don't know if I have been complimented, ridiculed or merely "tweaked." Probably all of the above, to a degree.

Most of the time it's as if I were on the New York City subway. No one makes eye contact unless it is someone you know or someone who wants, on this particular day, to know you. So I'm somewhat surprised to have a young, big, tough-looking gent lock his eyes on me as if they were heat-seeking radar and I were an enemy aircraft. I'm alone, on my way to get a fry bread taco at a food booth named, with typical Indian humor, not the "Red Lobster" but the "Rez Lobster." "What does this hulking brute have in mind?" I ask myself.

"I know you. You're that Wally McRae guy, ennit." (I probably should explain "ennit" since it isn't in your dictionary but is a common, all-purpose, universal, trans-tribal, reservation word that usually requests confirmation but sometimes is a question in itself. I kid the Alberta cowboy singer Ian Tyson by suggesting to him that Canadian Indians say, "Ennit. Eh?" I think you get the idea.)

Not being sure whether I have a critic or a fan, or whether he is asking or telling me my name, I answer, trying to keep it light but retaining the option to go either way, "I'm what's left of him."

"I thought it was you. You spoke at my uncle's funeral," he said.

"James King?" I asked.

"He was my uncle. I thought it was you, but all you white guys sorta look alike." (See how the tweaking works?) "Then I saw those red boots and I know for sure. It's sorta like having your name on your belt, ennit. You did a good job for my uncle."

"Thanks," I said, and we shook hands. I remembered to offer him an "Indian courteous" limp hand, while he responded with a respectful "White firm" handshake.

It was a good day. Or a good morning, at least. I almost got lost in the laid-back "Indian time" atmosphere visiting with Carl Braine, Roger Old Mouse, "Rabbit" Bearchum and others, but remembered that I had to get home, eat dinner, pick up Ruth and her picnic supper and head for the next event on our social calendar.

SHAKESPEAREAN THEATER

After spending most of the morning and part of the afternoon at the powwow, I came home and Ruth and I drove back by the forks of Lame Deer Creek and the powwow grounds and headed for Birney, or more precisely, Poker Jim Butte Fire Lookout Tower on the Ashland Division of the Custer National Forest, to watch Montana Shakespeare in the Parks, a touring theater group from Montana State University, perform *Love's Labour's Lost*, my second cultural event of the day.

The elaborate portable set used by the troupe is dwarfed by the natural setting atop Poker Jim Butte. Only the curvature of the Earth prevents one from seeing—as Henry Bailey once responded to the question of how far you can see from the top of that hill—"all the way to St. Paul." The Wolf Mountains, blue as a morning glory, are to the west. South of them, farther away, fainter but higher, are the Big Horns. And the rest of the compass points feature ponderosa, prairie, plains and mesas in a jumble of shapes, sizes and shades and varying hues, from the warm yellows of sandstone, the hot magenta and rose of the scoria and clinker divide tops, cooling to the greens of grass, juniper, and pines and finally the misty blues of distance and sky that blend together until there is no clearly defined horizon.

Except for the soft bawling of Irv Alderson's cattle and an occasional "L e t ' s g o s e e e e e old Hugo Fritz!" of meadowlark song, there is silence. Utter, complete, absolute silence.

It is an odd place to celebrate Shakespeare. The audience, by some counts, is just as odd because they sure don't look like your regular Shakespearean fans. Nearly all are, if not speaking, at least nodding, acquaintances. Most of the audience comes early, to visit or discover whom the few unknown faces belong to. No mystery or question is long in being answered and spread through those assembled. "That's Jean and Floyd Dahlman, from the Forsyth Flat." "That's Bart, the County Road Boss. Laurel the postmistress's husband, Butch, the road grader operator, must have invited him." "That's a politician from over in Big Horn County looking for votes."

The set, costumes, props and cast are trailered, and four-wheel-drive towed, nine torturous, steadily climbing miles on occasional gravel, but mostly dirt—with grass between the tracks—roads in the most primitive sense of the word.

Perhaps because of the morning's experience, I am struck by the thought that this is a vision-quest site and that the

Cheyennes and we are both in the wrong places and should switch spots. Each group is attempting to find their cultural roots, and yet each group is distracted by their surroundings. The Cheyennes are trapped in a hot, muggy, mosquito-infested valley, surrounded by exhaust fumes, public-address system squeals and firecrackers. We, on the other hand, are distracted from the magnificence of Shakespearean words, phrases and rhyme by our ethereal surroundings. Our eyes are drawn from the stage and the actors to the vastness of panoramic views, and our cultural trappings are almost intrusive in this wild and beautiful place.

When I can concentrate and follow the play, I am entertained by the wit of the words and by the ability of the actors, but—and this is my fault and not the cast's or the playwright's—I find myself unable to absorb the whole humor, and in the end, sensibility, of the play.

Of all the different venues at which the Shakespearean players perform, Poker Jim is their favorite. The audience appreciates the extra effort involved in getting to the site and staging the production. There are none of the usual distractions. No barking dogs or train or car horns interfere. The clean scents of pine and trampled grass are a welcome relief from the usual urban odors. But I come to the surprising conclusion that the sets, costumes, dialogue and acting are all diminished by the setting. If the theatrical company realized the power of nature's competition, perhaps Poker Jim would not be their favorite place to perform. They are upstaged by the pastoral panoramic setting. To me, the whole effort is nearly as obscure as the Cheyenne drummers' songs that I heard earlier in the day.

COUNTRY DANCE

Ruth and I ate our supper picnic atop Poker Jim Butte while the Shakespearean crew disassembled the set and packed the costumes for the return to civilization.

The Birney Shakespeare Club was having a fund-raising

dance at the old Birney Ranch Store that night and we felt we should support the effort with our presence and our purse. Our neighbors Bill and Dade Allison and their Three Rivers Band were providing the music, so there was an added reason to attend.

There was quite a bit of time to pass between supper and the dance. Although there were several obligatory offers to "come have supper with us and visit until the dance," we felt equally inclined to decline, knowing that we would, to a degree, at least, be imposing. Both the offer and the refusal are equal sides of the Cowboy Code equation that is so simple and at the same time confusing. Besides, we wanted to be alone and have a drive up Tongue River towards Sheridan, Wyoming, during the second-most beautiful time of the day.

We descended from Poker Jim and wound our way down the East Fork and the main Hanging Woman Creek to Birney and then up the Tongue. Butch had done a good job on the red scoria road, but we drove slowly. A family of African Americans was fishing from the Hanging Woman Bridge. A small black urchin emerged from behind their Colorado-licensed van and attempted to shoot a suction-tipped arrow at us from a yellow plastic bow. We all waved at one another, with the exception of the kid playing Indian trying to ambush us cowboys. Maybe a mile upriver from the bridge, a half dozen turkey vultures were just beginning their supper of a fresh road-killed marmot.

The Birney community has fascinated me all of my life. I have always lived close enough, and yet far enough away, to objectively study its unique culture and sociology. Each rural community is the same, and yet different. But Birney is much more different than most. Maybe that it was settled by highly educated and urbane, cultured people from the Deep South tended to make it more competitive and at the same time more civil than most western enclaves. Several things jump out at you about Birney: everyone has always known their "place" in the social pecking order; no one ever rocked the boat; and no community was as ingrained and steady. I was invited to be the speaker on two different occasions at the Birney School Eighth Grade Graduation, which is a big deal because there is no high school within striking distance, so the youth must leave home to attain schooling beyond the elementary level. Once when I was the speaker, each of the five graduates represented a minimum of five generations in that community! There are likely very few places, if any, where the same continuity of families exists.

Birney has always been a sort of Brigadoon or Camelot. For generations, it existed in a vacuum, somehow isolated and insulated from the rest of the world. During the thirties, forties and early fifties, dudes came, mostly from the East Coast, bringing needed income and intellectual stimulation, but they took away only a few photographs and the memory of a western ranch experience. I was performing poetry at Dartmouth College once and a sprightly lady, having found out that I was from Montana, came bustling up to me and said in her broad New England accent, "Montana? Ah, Montana. I bet I know a place in Montana to which you have never been." I know that she was disappointed that I not only knew Birney well, but she was saddened by my report that every local resident she remembered from her days in Birney was dead. She was clearly upset when I correctly guessed that she had spent her time in Birney at the Bones Brothers Ranch.

During the 1970s, however, the outside world finally discovered the Birney community. The "energy crisis" created a frenzy of interest by energy companies and speculators in sewing up "coal properties" through purchase or lease. The financial prospects from, and the sociological and environmental fears of, coal-oriented industrial development philosophically divided what was once a tight, cohesive community. The persuasive arguments of both the environmentalists and the speculators divided generations and families. It separated a hundred years of neighboring into warring factions and fostered bitter feuds.

As Ruth and I drove up the Tongue River, we reveled in

the beauty of the countryside, but as we ticked off the ranches sold, traded and leased for coal development, we grieved—the 4D, the Quarter Circle U, Knoblocks, the Three Circle and more. I recalled eloquent testimony from one of Birney's most prominent ranchers accusing opponents to coal development of being unpatriotic and remembered his patient explanation that coal development was the only solution to the ranchers' ever-increasing financial bind and that all could use those proffered coal dollars to improve and upgrade not only the livestock but the physical environment as well. He concluded in fine oratorical style: "We have inherited this wonderful resource, coal, from the dinosaurs. For whom are we saving it, the Martians?" At the entrance to the Double Circle Ranch, there is a large, colorful, routed sign with the Consolidation Coal Company logo "Consol" on it.

We drove thoughtfully back to the dance at the Ranch Store, as it was getting deep into dusk. The turkey buzzard diners at the marmot banquet had increased by four. The African American fishing family, including the bow-and-arrow-armed black "warrior," was gone.

The Three Rivers Band was tuning up and adjusting the sound when we got back to the stone-walled Birney Ranch Store. Both it and the Birney Cash Store were closed and empty of groceries, sundries and produce. The Corral Bar and Dance Hall had burned down some years ago for the second and last time; only the fireplace chimney and both foundations remained as a tombstone and grave markers. There was a huge, trailered cabin cruiser parked in front of one of the houses. Laurel and Butch Fjell were feeding barbequed hamburgers and the fixin's to the Shakespeare cast. Their daughter was selling dance and raffle tickets for a Gordon Alderson silver-mounted bridle bit on the porch of the store.

Inside the gutted hall, the mosquitoes were a bit less plentiful than outside. Ruth visited with Brenda and Sonny, whose mates were playing guitars and singing. Dade, the drummer, and Cody, the lead singer, were single. Little girls with toothless smiles, representing the sixth generation, danced together in their arm-wrenching version of the jitterbug, oblivious to the beat. The Forest Service firefighters from the Ft. Howe ranger station hung around outside on the porch looking for action, or prospects. Two older women danced together. The Shakespeare cast, full of Laurel's chuck and Butch's bullshit, came in and danced. I did an arthritic courtesy dance with Ruth as out of sync as the sixth generation and talked to a fifth-generation rancher, home for the Fourth of July to visit his widowed mother and his brother. He's managing the Beartooth Ranch out of Columbus these days. I asked him about the two benches, half-logs, round on the top, flat on the bottom, with spraddled legs mitered into the round side of the logs. "Why were they made that way? Where did they come from?"

"They used to sit on the porch of the store," John said, "—one on each side of the door. They made them round side up so the drunk Cheyennes couldn't sleep on them without falling off. Instead, they slept on the flat-topped benches up the street at the Cash Store."

The cast members of *Love's Labour's Lost* were from places like New York, North Carolina, Minneapolis, Albuquerque, Pocatello and Seattle. They reminded me of the eastern dudes enjoying their western ranch experience. But, like their dude predecessors, their style of dancing had not come in contact with true cowboy choreography. But they were having fun. As outsiders, undivided by the bitterness of the decades of rancor about coal development, they were free to enjoy the country dance, while most of the members of the Birney community could not.

There were no Indians, drunk or sober. They were still at the powwow, over the divide at the Forks of Lame Deer Creek, watching the Men's Fancy Dance Competition, I suppose.

TRESPASSING

Maybe every rancher has his own reason, or story. This is mine.

Deputy Sheriff Tom Skinner stopped at our house one evening and said, "I didn't think you were giving permission for camping on your place during the fire season."

"That's right, Tom," I replied.

"Well, I just cut across from Tongue River on the county road and someone is setting up a camp at your Bickle Well."

"Who the hell is it?"

"I don't know. Didn't stop. Thought I better check with you first." I told Tom that I would head over there and asked if he wanted to come with me. "I think that would be a good idea," Tom said. "Sometimes these misdemeanors on the part of the trespassers turn into felonies perpetrated by the affected landowner."

By the time we got to the Bickle Well, although light was still lingering in the western sky, it was dark. Sure enough, a tent, a small travel trailer, a camper and other assorted crap were drawn into a circle like a sloppy pioneer wagon train. I'm fuming. Tom knows it. "Don't make me shoot you," he cautions.

I trace a flashlight beam to the hand holding it. "Just what in the hell do you think you're doing?" I ask, in a tone that to me seems fairly under control, considering the circumstances.

"Easy," Tom says.

"I'm looking for my toothpaste," a feminine voice shakily replies.

"Toothpaste? Toothpaste!" I holler, "Who the hell gave you permission to brush your goddam teeth on my outfit?"

Tom grabs my arm as the voice says, "I don't know. I just work here," which makes no sense to either Tom or me. "Larry is in the camper."

"Who's Larry?" Tom asks in a kind and considerate voice before I can further pursue my perfectly logical line of questioning.

"Larry's the boss," the quavering voice replies.

I regain the floor with "Who the hell is Larry?"

"What's going on out there?" a booming voice breaks in from the direction of the pickup camper.

"Are you a son of a bitch named Larry?" I reasonably inquire.

"Who wants to know?" the camper voice replies.

"Everybody just calm down and shut up," Tom says. "Just shut the hell up. I'll ask the questions. You! Go brush your teeth. Larry could you get out of the camper and come over here? I'm going to turn the headlights on and we'll straighten this out."

It turns out that Larry has a "Dr." in front of his name and is an archaeologist with a contract to hunt for artifacts for the Bureau of Land Management prior to the granting of a federal coal lease. Dr. Larry assumed that since the BLM had hired him, either he was on federal land or the bureau had contacted me, the surface owner. I pointed out that while the coal under the surface might be owned by the federal government, or the Burlington Northern Railroad, he and his crew were camped, and brushing their teeth, on somebody else's land, namely mine. And that he really needed, damn quickly, to get the hell off it.

"It's dark," Dr. Larry pleaded, "Where am I going to go at this time of night."

"Somewhere off this outfit, and don't let your shirttail touch your back doin' it," I suggested.

Dr. Larry and his crew started packing up. "You're leaving then?" Tom asked.

"I don't think I have any choice," Dr. Larry replied, eyeing the look on my face as well as Tom's badge and sidearm.

As we were leaving, Tom asked, "Are you satisfied, now?"

"Not by a damn sight," I fired back, "I want to file trespass charges."

"I don't think it'll do you any good."

"Why the hell not? The son of a bitch was trespassing."

"I didn't see any sign at the gate we came through from the county road. And he wasn't hunting big game. The justice of the peace won't accept the charge if you file it, unless you told Larry that he didn't have permission to be on your ranch before coming onto your outfit."

"I never saw the bastard before in my life. How could I tell him?"

"Did you have a sign up?"

"Hell, I don't know. Maybe he tore it down when he went through the gate."

"Can you prove it?" Tom asked. He was correct, of course. The J.P. wouldn't accept my filing charges because no law had been broken.

"The guy was trespassing," Tom said, "but it was pretty innocent. Why do you guys all go off like a skyrocket when someone, like this rock picker, wanders onto your land without permission?"

"I don't know."

"Well, if you ever figure it out, explain it to me because I just don't understand. "

Just lately, our son, Clint, called and reported that he had seen signs of someone trespassing on our outfit. Clint didn't have time to check it out but someone had parked their camper-topped pickup, with maps spread out on the passenger seat, along the Lay Creek-Greenleaf road. By the time I got gathered up, the suspect was maybe five miles farther north, parked again, but within the fenced right-of-way.

You can get a lot of information just by reading license plates in Montana. An out-of-state license indicates either a hunter or a confused tourist. Either state or U.S. government plates usually translate into bad news. The Montana citizens' license plates identify the county of the vehicle owner. The more populated counties were given lower numbers, so a low county number indicates a more urban driver, which quickly translates into a negative driver profile. It's really pretty simple. The number 1 guarantees trouble, as do all of the first seven, in descending order. But drivers of vehicles with county designations higher than 50 probably deserve an invitation to your next meal to gossip about horse hay, yearling steer prices the effects of beef packer concentration on the market and mutual acquaintances.

The suspect pickup bore "5" plates, which immediately pegged the driver in the worst 10 percent. Further points could be subtracted for the hailed-out appearance of the pickup, the camper on the back and especially the presence of maps.

The driver was hunkered down alongside the red scoria road when I drove up. "Are you having trouble?" I asked, which, translated in cowboy country, means, "What are you doing?"

"No. No trouble at all," which meant that the driver was unacquainted with the subtle translation required of ranchland queries, and his failure further lowered his already dismal driver quotient.

"Can I help you? Do you need a lift?" I ask the previous question again, in a slightly different way.

"No. Thanks for stopping, though."

Which requires me to counter his verbal chess move with a more direct approach that violates one of the minor tenets of the West, "What are you doing?"

Turns out he is a botanist with a summer contract looking for "pristine prairie habitat" for some do-gooder organization.

We had an interesting conversation about the effect of cattle grazing, and other agricultural practices, on prairie ecology. Finally, erroneously believing that I was a reasonable person, and with a tacit acknowledgement of his recent up-the-road trespassing sin, he asked, "Why is all the land in this part of the country posted against trespassing?"

I gave the stock answers: "fire, weed introduction, poaching, surveying for coal-related activities"—you know the list. But then, for some reason, I thought back to Deputy Tom's question of my irrational ire at innocuous trespassing and I tried to explain the real reason. "It's a statement of pride of ownership and control over a certain piece of real estate. Those signs say 'This is mine. I own this. I have responsibilities, an investment, and love for this property. I may choose to share it with you, but this is mine.'"

★ ★ ★

My grandfather John B. McRae left his home in Scotland in 1882 and traveled under canvas sails to Brownsville, Texas. He worked his way north—I'd like to claim with a Texas trail herd, but that isn't true—to Montana, which was just opening up for livestock grazing settlement. He worked on several fledgling ranches on the Tongue River and at the head of Rosebud Creek. He wanted to be a rancher; he wanted to own livestock. And he yearned to own something that was impossible to acquire in Scotland—land! In order to be a rancher, the first step was to get some livestock, run them on free government land and use those grazing animals to attain his ultimate goal. He frugally saved his wages in order to purchase a small band of sheep.

Sheep were animals that from his native land he knew well, understood, and until he died, loved.

My grandfather's timing could not have been worse. He bought the sheep in the fall of 1886. The winter of '86 and '87 was a killer. Charlie Russell painted his small watercolor of a starving cow, surrounded by opportunistic wolves, that winter and titled it *Waiting for a Chinook* or *The Last of 5000*.

A friend of my grandfather's became concerned during the course of the winter, rented a couple of saddle horses from Lazenby's Livery Barn in Rosebud and, riding one horse and leading the other, struck out through the drifts towards the Rosebud Buttes where he believed that his friend John B. was ranging with the sheep. Finally, coming across the tracks of sheep and a man afoot, he followed their meandering trail. Along the way he found skinned sheep carcasses and, cached in the tops of ponderosa pines, sheep pelts.

When he overtook the dwindling band, the friend told my grandfather, "I brought this horse for you to ride back to the settlement. Come with me."

"And leave the sheep? I can't do that. They're all I own in the world."

"John, the sheep are going to die. All of them. And if you don't come with me you're going to die too."

"When the last sheep dies," Grandfather told his friend, "I'll be here to skin it."

When spring finally came, he gathered and sold the sheep pelts and, with the money, bought 160 acres of unsurveyed "script" land from a French-Canadian trapper, prospector and squatter. That sheep pelt purchase was the beginning of the McRae Ranch.

I have not forgotten.

KAHARSKI HOMESTEAD

Although I was a usually responsible ten-year-old, I must have ignored the gnaw of guilt. I didn't report my destination to my mother when I left the house on that particular day. Having explored most of the easily reached intriguing places within a short ride of the home place, I trespassed onto a neighboring ranch, never knowing I would later own that piece of land. I caught, bridled and saddled Snooper. (How my father must have regretted allowing me to name him.) Maybe I was older, or younger, than ten. But I must have been tall and strong enough to open the tight barbed wire gates into, and out of, the Cemetery Pasture, gaining access to Josh McCuistion's outfit.

Snooper and I were ideally suited. The Welsh-cross gelding my dad bought after Bisco Spottedwolf retired him from the rodeo arena was of just the right size and disposition for a kid. He was old enough and wise enough to keep me, and himself, out of trouble. My new secondhand Furstnow saddle fit the physical scale of horse and rider so that from a distance we could be mistaken for a full-size cowboy and mount.

Responding to my complaint that the leather horn cover was worn through to the rawhide on the saddletree, my father slapped the fresh scrotum of a short-yearling bull over the horn and tied it on with a length of cotton string until it shrunk and became a permanent part of the saddle. Even though I was warned to keep my right hand away from the horn as I rode, I would dreamily caress the soft scrotal hair until it was worn away.

After leaving our Cemetery Pasture, we headed east. Half a mile into McCuistion's pasture, I could see the abandoned homestead. Upon sighting the buildings, I realized that I had seen the place before. While trailing some of our yearlings across Josh's ranch, we had watered them at a reservoir up Miller Creek from the buildings. "That was the Kaharski Place," my dad answered to my query. "That's where I heard a radio for the first time. Mr. Kaharski was pretty progressive and always kept up with new inventions. I rode over there to visit them once and they had just got a crystal set. Mr. Kaharski tuned the radio and handed me the earphones as the rest of the family sat around and watched my reaction. Some guy was singing 'The Preacher and the Bear' on the radio. It was like a miracle."

Snooper, taking one look at the cattails, swamp grass and pools of water, refused to even consider crossing the creek. After detouring the boggy stretch, I finally found a crossing that Snooper deemed safe and we approached the weathered buildings of the homesite.

Goosing and shying at the abandoned machinery and buildings, my horse eventually settled down enough for me to dismount and hobble him amid the milling blackbirds, clicking out their warnings to us intruders, and swarming deerflies greedy for our blood.

Before entering the house, I remembered a story my dad had repeated of an incident Josh McCuistion experienced on the trail up from Texas involving another abandoned dwelling.

"One night a hydrophoby skunk snuck up and bit one of the trail hands in the face while he was in his bedroll. He screamed and woke up the rest of us in the crew. They was enough light to see the skunk dragging his tail around

on the ground like a laying hen with an egg broke in her. One of the hands dispatched the skunk with a handy piece of firewood. We all knew what the deal was—including the guy from Arkansas who got bit. 'Shoot me now,' he pleaded, 'I know I'm gonna die anyway. Don't let me suffer. A man can't survive the hydrophoby.'"

"'Maybe the skunk didn't have it. He might a'been sick with something else.'"

"'It might be that you won't git it,' someone else suggested."

"'Let's see what happens, before we do anything' the boss said."

"'Sweet Jesus, we know what's gonna happen,' Arkansas pleaded. 'Shoot me now, so's I don't have to suffer.' But none of us had the grit to shoot him. But we kept the firearms well hid and watched him real close for a few days and, sure enough, he come down with it."

"When we saw he wasn't gonna git over it and was gittin' worse, we come on an abandoned cabin. So rather than put him out of his misery, me and another guy roped him around the waist and led him to the cabin and put him in it. We nailed the door shut real tight so he couldn't git out. Lord God Almighty, I can still hear his screams as we rode away. I wish to hell one of us could a' shot him."

I knew whose homestead this had been. My dad, while describing the wonders of the crystal set radio, had called it "The Ka *Horse* key Place." His locally practiced mispronunciation honed my curiosity. There must be some remainder left of the horses once there. There were no skunks in sight. The dug-in-the-bank, south-facing barn was empty. The house was filled with all sorts of interesting things, but if there was a radio with batteries and headphones attached, I didn't find it. If I had discovered the radio I'm sure I would have left it there. I may have been a trespasser, but I was not a thief. There were scores of old magazines lying around, *American, Colliers, Liberty* and *Country Gentleman* emblazoned on the curled and tattered covers. After looking through them, I left everything as I had found it, unhobbled Snooper, remounted, skirted the boggy creek and rode home. Upon returning, my mother asked, "What have you been doing for so long?"

"Riding," I said.

"Where did you go?"

"No place," I said.

★ ★ ★

After buying the McCuistion ranch from Josh's son, the new owner, Jack Higham, spent the next ten years "improving the place." Jack erected a white painted board fence at the ranch entrance. He fixed other pasture fences, accurately bragging about setting "twenty-eight thousand Penta-treated posts." He developed more livestock water and hay meadows and planted and cultivated government-sponsored shelter belts on the gumbo flats. The neighbors viewed these progressive changes with mixed emotions. Perhaps, had Jack been a native in the community, there would not have been nearly unanimous local disapproval of his "cleaning up" all of the remnants of the homesteads. "One of those old shacks that Jack 'dozed up and burned would look pretty cozy if a man was caught out there in a blizzard," a neighbor would rationalize.

The real roots of their criticism had much more to do with the erasure of visual reminders of past friends and neighbors. The locals' unspoken protestations refuted the western myth of the hostility ranchers had towards the homesteaders. Homesteaders might be jokingly referred to as "honyockers" and pitied for their naiveté, but they were not the enemy. The guilty parties—the federal government and the railroads that enticed the homesteaders to bet their lives in futile attempts to farm a hostile land—were the enemies.

After owning the ranch for ten years, Jack Higham died. I sold my interest in the ranch where I was raised and bought out Jack's widow. We graze two-year-old heifers on what was once the Kaharski Homestead.

Last week, my son, daughter-in-law and two of our granddaughters dug around in the Kaharski dump, returning with a treasure of old medicine and beer bottles and the right arm of a porcelain doll.

"Whose place was that? What happened to them? Where did they go? Why did they leave?" our granddaughters asked me. I told them some of the story as well as I could.

TALKING BRANDS

The Big Sky Cafe is a trailer house diner on Front Street in Forsyth. You might never have been in it, but you've been in one that's a whole lot like it. You know, one of those places where the railroad and county retirees hang out with the ranch locals and swap opinions and rumors. If you order a "Gut Bomb," which isn't on the menu, that's okay. Deb—owner, waitress and cook—will fix up a Big Sky Burger, which is a double-ought cheeseburger with chili and a quarter inch of raw onion on top. It's a good place. The seating is limited to three or four small tables and a few stools at the counter. Unless there is a family, or a woman customer, you sit at the first available seat; even if you don't know the neighbors, it's okay—you'll get acquainted. It's that kind of an establishment.

I went in there a while back and there was an open seat beside Owen Badgett. Owen was just finishing a bait of side pork and must have lonelied out up on the flats above Ingomar and came to town less to eat, but more to visit. Owen is a damn fine poetry reciter and a semi-pro storyteller. I sat down and ordered two, over easy, a short stack and bacon. Owen wants to talk brands. We begin with some of the old ones, the F U F,

C B C, X I T and some of those. "Why did lots of those early-day outfits that had their choice of brands choose a three-figure one?" I wondered out loud.

"That's an easy one," Owen answers. "Damn hard to run a three-iron brand into something else if you're so inclined."

That just naturally segued into examples of brands that could be either mistaken or rearranged. I cited Anna Grace Davidson's walking Y Bar Box (connected) and Garfield's walking Y Bar D (connected), both on the left rib, as an example that even Pat Graham or Grant Gatlin of the State Brand Office couldn't separate 100 percent of the time. They didn't exactly neighbor, but the outfits weren't that far apart, being within fifteen miles apart on the Rosebud. Then there's Brewster's bowl up Quarter Circle over a U, on the left hip, and the old Dowlin mark, which by adding to the Quarter Circle U a couple of opposite facing wings on the top of the U and a bar underneath you had Dowlin's Quarter Circle Seven U Seven Bar.

When it was Owen's turn, he ripped a couple of napkins out of the dispenser, whipped out his #2 Dixon Ticonderoga tallying pencil and proceeded to sit right there in the Big Sky Cafe and steal damn near half of the cattle in eastern Montana. I mean, he was making me nervous. So I dropped out of the conversation.

Owen changes the direction then. "Where do you put that Coat Hanger brand of yours on a critter? What do you call it?"

"Rocker Six," I says. "Mostly on the left hip, although I have it recorded on the left rib and hip both. Why?"

"Just wondering. You can tell a lot about a guy by the position of a brand," and he's off at a lope. "You qualify as a true cowman. Where do you brand a horse?"

"Same brand, right thigh."

"Damn!! I never would have guessed it, but you're a horseman too."

I was complimented, but confused. "How do you figure?"

"It's like I was telling you, you can tell the man by the place of the brand. Now most heelers are right handed. Right?"

"Yah," I say.

"So if the heeler only connects on one leg, which one will it be?"

"Chances are it'll be the off one. Right hind leg. So?"

"So if the wrestlers don't have their head in their ass, they trip the calf across the rope and therefore the left side ends up and you don't have to roll him over. Right?"

"Guess I never thought about it. But yah, you're right."

"But now take a colt," Owen continues, "You don't heel him do you? Hell no! You neck him unless you're one of those buckaroo types that are long on fancy loops and fashion. Then the mugger, being normally right handed like the calf heeler, goes down the rope and puts the holt on him, twists him down, and the right side ends on the sunny side."

I'm beginning to see the logic in all of this, for the first time. But the learning process continues: "So where does a purebred breeder brand?"

"Easy!" I think, "On the left."

"No! He wants to save that spot for the commercial cowman that's gonna buy his bull. Chances are he's gonna brand in a chute, or on a table where it doesn't make any difference, so he brands that purebred on the right, someplace."

"Makes sense," I concede.

"Where does the novice, backyard, twenty-three-acre horse person want his, or her, brand to go, then?"

"Hell, I don't know," I say. "Where?"

"On the left shoulder. It's the only place they feel safe around a horse."

"How about the farmer? Where does a farmer plant his stamp?"

"I'll bite." I said.

"Down low on the right belly." Owen snorts, "That way he can look over from his stool as he's juicing his Jersey and say,

'Yes sir! By damn, she's mine all right! All mine.'"

Feeling that the lesson is about over, I ask Owen, "Where do you brand your horses?"

"Left neck," he says.

Try as I might, I can't figure that one. Owen has laid his trap for my question, "Why on the left neck?"

"I don't yearn to be easily classified," Owen says. "I guess that I'm maybe the last cowboy iconoclast."

RICHARDSON'S
REVENGE

Okay, call me an insensitive clod, or a bully if you like. But, frankly, Richardson somehow managed to really get on my nerves. Part of the problem came from the deferential treatment that he received from the other members of the Sigma Chi fraternity at Montana State. I'm sure the other members of my fraternity felt Lee Richardson had experienced a tough go and was, therefore, to be treated with kindness and understanding. He had some sort of a congenital spinal defect and, in order to fix the problem, an orthopedic specialist had removed several vertebrae. As a result, although his legs and the rest of his body were of normal size, the operation rendered him unnaturally short. He was also extremely skinny and sort of sickly and had a diabolical laugh, a taunting nature and a grating voice.

My high school science teacher probably had a role in influencing my callous treatment of Richardson. Mr. Russell once gave us a biology assignment requiring the class members to find a current news article relating to some aspect of animal issues. Collin Wilsey, one of my classmates, gave a newspaper report on a person whose mission was to collect birds with broken wings, nurse them back to physical wholeness and return them to the wild. Collin was a gentle spirit, and although the report was a bit smarmy, the class consensus was that she had done well.

Mr. Russell, however, went into one of his patented educational tirades. "That is probably one of the most misguided, soft-headed ideas to ever surface on the face of the earth!" Mr. Russell exploded. "First of all, why does a bird get the broken wing? Did it stupidly fly into a telephone line? Is this an avian example of faulty eyesight? You reported that some of the birds were ducks shot by hunters. Why are many *other* ducks able to avoid hunters in poorly camouflaged blinds? Do the ducks this idiot revives suffer from genetic flaws? And is it possible that this do-gooder is so perpetuating weak genes that one day all ducks will have such weak wings that they will be forced to *walk* south in the fall? What are the evolutionary results? What do we know about the law of unintended consequences?" It was a masterful combination of theatrics and science so typical of Mr. Russell.

I probably thought that once Richardson's back had been repaired he should have been treated like everyone else and suffer the rough-and-tumble treatment the rest of us were subject to.

The stage play and subsequent film *Tea and Sympathy* could have added to my apparent insensitivity. Although unfounded, the young man in *Tea and Sympathy* was somehow thought to have homosexual tendencies. His friends overprotected him to such an extent that he began to question his masculinity and worth as a human. The wife of the Dean of Students, sensing the young man's precarious mental state, seduced him, therefore restoring faith in his manliness. Greek tragedy. Happy ending.

Whatever the rationalization or excuse, I treated Richardson like shit. As pledge trainer I assigned him the most miserable assignments.

He didn't date, that I recall, nor did he participate in the fraternity keg parties indulged in by most of us. Studying and masterfully playing Lee Swan's Hammond organ were his major activities. He was an excellent student in the pre-medicine program. "Richardson, you certainly don't expect to ever become a medical doctor do you?" I challenged. "Your grades might qualify you for medical school, but surely you realize that you will never be able to handle it, or the ordeal of internship. You just aren't tough enough. I think you should switch over to agriculture and become a brochure-pushing county extension agent or something like that."

Years later, someone asked Richardson if it was tough becoming a doctor. Lee shook his head and replied, "A lot harder than I imagined. I never would have made it, but I kept remembering what that damn Wally McRae said and I stuck with it just to spite him. He's one of the reasons I'm a doctor today."

Flash forward: several years later, Dr. Richardson is a general practitioner in Laurel, Montana. I am struggling to keep a ranch together while managing to break my left leg three times in six years in various horse wrecks. The second time a horse fell on me, the doctor in Miles City tried to get the bones close enough together to heal by manipulating the plaster cast. It wasn't working. The bones kept slipping as the muscles in my leg atrophied. It was finally decided that I should be operated on by an orthopedic surgeon in Billings. Dr. Hagen would use a couple of stainless steel screws and a bone graft to make the separated ends of the big bone in my leg knit together.

The morning of the scheduled surgery I was prepped, given a shot of Demerol and wheeled into the operating room. And who should I see there? Why, it's Dr. Richardson, resplendent in his green scrubbies with a surgical mask dangling rakishly from around his scrawny neck. "Well, McRae. It's so nice to see you," he says.

I'm flying in a drug-induced cloud of Demerol. I don't give a damn about anything. "Richardson, you little cold-fingered creep, whose body are you violating today?" I inquire.

"Yours," he answers with a diabolical giggle.

"Like shit, you are," I reply, "Dr. Hagen is my doctor."

"Dr. Hagen will do the main surgery and he will do a good job. I know because he's the one that fixed my spine and inspired me to become a doctor." (Not giving me any credit whatsoever, despite what I had learned via the rumor mill.) "I found out you were scheduled for surgery today and Dr. Hagen, knowing of our past relationship, invited me to scrub in and take the bone out of your pelvic arch for the graft," he chuckled.

"You stay away from me and my pelvic arch—you aren't my doctor. If you even touch any part of my body close to my pelvis I swear I'll sue your ass."

"I just hope you're tough enough to stand the pain," he chortles.

"Pain?" I quake.

"Drilling the holes and the actual screwing of the bones together will only cause you minor discomfort," he says, as if he had practiced the line from the medical practitioner's script. "We'll be able to control that with drugs. Unfortunately, where I take the bone out for the graft is another matter. Have you been told about that procedure?" and he giggles again.

Hesitantly I reply, "I don't think so."

"Do you have a power-driven grindstone back home on the ranch?"

I nod.

"Basically, that's what I'll use after I cut a slit just to the left of your crotch with a scalpel and retract the overlying tissue and muscle using a device with sharp teeth—like the spreader they use in the tire shops—which grasps and holds the incision open. The grinder sounds something like this," and he vocally demonstrates the sound of a grindstone under heavy resistance. "We won't use an actual piece of bone. I will catch the mushy, bloody chips and shavings, then pack the material around the repaired break in the tibia somewhat like you would use grout. It's relatively simple. There's only one drawback."

"What's that?"

"Oh, it's minor. It's the post-op pain. When you come out of the general anesthesia you won't feel much pain in your leg. Unfortunately, there will be a searing, pulsating, throbbing, shooting pain in what remains of your pelvis. There's really not much we can do about it. I guess you'll just have to grit your way through it."

"You're kidding," I say.

"Not at all. I want you to recall the time you locked me in the laundry chute in the basement of the Sigma Chi house and then poured bucket after bucket of cold water down on me from the third-floor attic—I'm sure you remember. Then every time your heart beats and you experience the excruciating, cadenced pain, I want you to repeat to yourself, 'Richardson did this. Richardson did this.' . . . I'll slip in and check on you tomorrow. Okay?"

He was right about the pain. He did drop in the next day. My leg healed as good as new. Richardson and his wife, Irma, are valued members of the Laurel community. And I guess I can take some pride in having influenced Dr. Lee Richardson's becoming a much-loved family doctor and general practitioner in Yellowstone County, Montana.

NEW NEIGHBORS

No one ever made a decent living on what my dad called the old Barringer Place. Well, maybe back in the early days when old man Barringer ran sheep free on government land the outfit might have made some money. I don't really know. Dad called it the Barringer Place, but you could just as accurately put any number of names on that same piece of real estate.

Frank Levi called it the Grooms Place, when he told about delivering the mail horseback to Ashland during the winter of 1919. "Yes, sir," Frank would recollect, "some Texans named Grooms leased it and brought some little, thin-hided, southern steers north into the country that fall. Me? I'd gambled away every damn thing I had. Didn't own enough clothes to flag a railroad hand car with, I didn't. There wasn't no jobs, 'cept this one, packing the mail up the Rosebud, then over the divide to Tongue River, so I took it. Damn near froze every day, all winter. Oh, I'd be okay on the 'Bud and the Tongue. There was enough outfits scattered along there so's I could thaw out every few miles. I'd back up and take a run at gettin' warm at Seymour Brown's place, but the chinook never lasted very long, I'll tell ya. Once I hit the top of the divide, it'd get pretty damn brisk as I struck that down slope towards the river. By the time I hit those flats on Lay Creek, I'd be near froze, so I'd get off, picket my horse to a plum bush and start in tailing up those sorry steers. They was so weak, from hollow belly and the cold, that they couldn't get up on their own. So I'd help them. They killed all the brush that winter since that's all they had to eat. Next spring you could walk for maybe two miles steppin' only on the carcasses, if you had a mind to, never touching the ground. I always figgered those steers kept me alive that winter of '19. Wish I could have done the same for them." Frank Levi was the only one I ever knew that called it the Grooms Place. I guess that terrible winter of '19 etched it forever in his mind.

Some referred to it as the Horton, but others might call it by other names: Andersons' or Mobleys' or, finally, Uricks'. In fact, you could sort of date a person's time in the neighborhood by whatever name they called it.

It never was a happy place. Maybe it has too much irrigation—around a thousand acres—without a balancing amount of grass. But there's more to it than that. Somewhere there is—or if not, should be—a written-down equation or theorem that explains that the direct application of irrigation water to land produces three things: lush crops, hard work and bitter people. As a general rule, irrigated farmers hate everyone upstream, dislike everyone downstream and everybody else can just go to hell. At one time I thought this bitterness was part of the whole farm culture, and that if you'd strip off their gum-soled shoes, seed corn caps and bibs with a hammer loop on the right pant leg, then replace those with Wilson boots, Levi's and a Resistol hat, they would develop more empathy for others of their kind. Then it dawned on me that wheat farmers get along and help one another pretty well. No, there's something culturally poisoning in irrigation water.

Everyone always said that it—I'll call it the Mobley Place, since I neighbored with them for years—had "lots of potential," whatever that means. But there was also a joking opinion that the only way that you could make the Mobley Place work was to bring back the days of slavery. It was a joke that no one thought was funny but used to explain the outfit. Part of the problem with this particular place has always been the lack of a close market for irrigated farm products. You can't haul sugar beets halfway across the country to a beet dump. The hay market is up and down. The same can be said for the gummer cow and the feeder bull deal. As Frank Levi testified, the winter wind blows either up or down the river, so it's not a good place for a feedlot. But it's not just economics. I suspect that even if it cranked money out like the Denver Mint it would produce little satisfaction, let alone joy.

A few years back, Urick bought it from Mobleys, but he stayed only long enough to get in some basic disagreements with his upriver neighbors, similar to the one his predecessor, Herb Mobley, got in with Buck Brien about the dam. The upriver rock dam had one advantage: it raised the river level enough to get the water into a gravity ditch, eliminating the high cost of pumping. But the dam also had a couple of disadvantages. Nearly every year, when the ice went out, the flood raised hell with the rock dam. The huge rocks that formed the diversion would tumble downriver and have to be replaced. Further, all the dam checking and repair had to be done from the banks on Mobley's upriver neighbor James Robinson's holdings on the Cheyenne Reservation. James Robinson had problems of his own. Moonlight lovers and persons looking for a place to imbibe a case or two of Bud Light frequently used the road to Herb's dam. To these folks, closing the gate along the public road was not a high priority, so James's cattle frequently found their way onto the highway.

James's father-in-law, Buck Brien, was a big, D9Cat of a man with scarred knuckles and a bad back, who had recently retired after a distinguished career as an Indian Reservation policeman. Buck lived in some diggings on Robinson's ranch, close to the frequently left-open gate. James instructed Buck to be his rep on the problem, a responsibility that Buck accepted with great enthusiasm, since he was sort of missing his glory days as a tough reservation cop.

One day, after the river ice went out, Herb Mobley stopped by on his way home from Ashland to check on the annual damage to his dam. While Herb was there, making mental notes on the needed repairs, a car came down the highway, screeched to a stop, backed up and came in the gate that Herb had, conveniently, just left open. Buck drove up, slowly extricated himself from his vehicle, checked all around for possible signs of ambush, and said, in a voice of official authority, "What the hell you doin' here?"

"Checking the dam."

"Why?"

"Why? Because it's my dam. That's why."

"This is James Robinson's."

"This may be Robinson's land, but that's my dam."

"You left the gate open," Buck accused.

"I'll shut it when I leave," Herb said, turning his back and having no idea who this intimidating individual was. The whole time Herb had been in the country, Buck had been over on the Crow, or maybe down on the Pine Ridge or Rosebud Reservation instructing respect for the law using his unique head-thumping methods.

"You forgot when you came in. You might forget again when you leave. Go shut it now," Buck challenged.

"Who the hell are you, anyway?" Herb asked.

"I'm Brien."

Herb knew that the Briens and Robinsons were related, and had heard that James Robinson's father-in-law had just come back to the country. "You got a first name, Brien?"

"Yeah. Buck. You got a name too?"

"I'm Mobley."

"Huh, Mobley. You got a first name, Mobley?"

"Herb."

"Herb. Herb Mobley," Buck pondered. "I never heard of anybody named Herb. The only Mobley I hear people speak of, in this country, is a guy named 'Chickenshit Mobley.' Is that you?"

Herb had related the story to me and told me, "I didn't know what to do. I figured that I had age on my side, while he had size. If I whipped him people would say that I picked on an old man. And he just might be the winner in a fight. He was wrong, but in a way, he was right. We stood there for a while and I finally said, 'I'm done here. Let's both leave. You go ahead. I'll shut the gate behind us.' I guess I did the right thing."

So Herb sold to Urick, and Urick ran into some of the same problems that everyone else had experienced on this hard-luck place for over a hundred years. I think everyone was surprised when it sold again. We all wondered who would be the victim this time, then we heard about the new owners.

All of the perceived concerns about the new neighbors— the customs, language, modes of transportation, dress, beliefs and culture—were certainly true. Families—large families— started moving in and building new houses all over the place. Semi truckloads of strange equipment showed up. And horses. Truckloads of heavy draft horses. The newcomers hauled in tons of harness, buggies, horse-drawn farming equipment from three generations past and hand tools. They were Amish.

Motivated mostly by curiosity, but rationalizing that I was exercising country courtesy, I went over to meet and greet the new neighbors. Urick was still there, getting his plunder gathered for his move to a new place in Oklahoma, and greeted me first.

"How's the new folks?" I asked.

"Okay, I guess. Sure different, though."

"Having any problems with them?"

"Well, they cut off the electricity and the telephone in our house and I had to get them hooked up again until we leave. And sometimes they speak German amongst themselves and

I don't know what they're saying about me. But I think they'll be okay."

About that time, a rangy bay trotted up from the fields down by the river, pulling a black buggy. The driver, looking like something out of the last century, or a costumed movie character, got down from his rig and hitched the bay's halter rope to a power pole.

"Ve gates, landsman," I said, using better than half of the German words I knew.

It was a mistake. The driver, assuming that I knew other German words as well, started rattling off a regular oration in a lingo that was foreign to me in the most basic sense of the word. I finally, after trying "No comprende," "Non parlez-vous France" and "No deutsch sprechen," got the whoa put on that foolishness and we got switched over to English, to his disappointment and my relief.

Urick made the introductions and the man and I palavered some. "My wife is from Pennsylvania," I said. "There are lots of Amish there."

"Oh, yah. Dat be Lancaster County den?"

"No. She's from Clinton County."

"Oh, yah. Dat land in Lancaster and York and dere, it be, you know tree tousand, maybe four tousand and so ve go vest."

"So, is that where you're from? Pennsylvania?"

"Oh, no. Ve go vest to vere your vife from first. Then to Illinois and Iova and den dat land it be the same, tree tousand, tree tousand five hundred, and there be more of us all the time. So ve go to Visconsin and den dat land it be den too high again. You know? So ve come here. I come from Visconsin. Yah, dat's vere ve come from, Visconsin. Because land here it not be dat high. You know? And it be so crowded and people coming in and roads and all dat. So ve come here, Montana. Maybe here ve keep our vays, not mit all dat English, you know? But ve be good neighbors."

I ventured a joke, "I see a trend developing. If you keep

moving west to get away from all of the high-priced land and the congestion, pretty soon you're going to run into the Pacific Ocean. What're you gonna do then?"

He got the joke. "I don't know. I tink maybe ve farm dat ocean, you know, start fishing."

We both laughed and talked about other things. He was concerned because it was April and they needed to be plowing, but an early spring storm had dumped several feet of drifted snow all over the fields. "They be ploughing back in Visconsin. Ve need to be doing dat."

As I was driving back to the county road, I considered their prospects. And I hoped that, somehow, they could make this historically unhappy piece of land work for them. But what would they raise? How would they get their products sold? Would this be a refuge from the escalating land prices, from the crowding, congestion and confinement that they fled? Or could they, by substituting hard work for technology and human and equine calories for BTUs, be happy and prosperous in their cultural definitions of those words? Suddenly, popping into my mind, was the old, bad joke about hard places like this requiring slave labor.

Just before I reached the gravel county road, I noticed a young Amish girl—maybe eleven years old—in one of the fields. She was—head thrown back, looking skyward, arms extended—twirling through the intermittent drifts of snow. The land, the sky, the drifts and the girl all in shades of black, white and gray. Oblivious to my presence, the girl spun as if caught in a series of old black-and-white photographs. And the words of Dr. Martin Luther King Jr. came to mind: "Free at last! Free at last! Thank God Almighty, we are free at last!"

HENRY

I know that you're going to think that I'm just piquing your more base inclinations, or hyping the story, when I tell you that there is an aspect, or a portion, of this recollection that is anatomically graphic and therefore probably offensive.

Aha! I was correct in thinking that you would stick with me. But you have been warned. Remember that.

Originally he didn't have a name. Naming him "Henry" came later. No, in the beginning he was just another steer calf, but sort of scruffy. Bull-sale auctioneers used to call his color "mellow yellow" as if it was a good thing when a bovine beast lacked any other distinguishing characteristics to recommend it. He was sort of frosty yellow but his hair coat looked as if he had been a breech birth that stayed that way, or like he was right in the middle of having a bad hair year. You know what I mean.

When we gather in the fall, we throw the herd together and sort the cattle three ways. The first cut is the "steers to go" and their mothers. The second cut, which we put in another pasture, is the "heifers to go" and their mothers. And the final cut—or what's left—is made up of the cows with replacement heifer calves, bulls, strays, drys and anything else that is not to be shipped as part of the calf contract. Then, on shipping day, the contracted calves, already sorted for sex, are separated from their mothers, loaded onto two-ton ranch trucks and goose-neck trailers, hauled to the scale, weighed, loaded onto livestock semitrailers and sent to their new home. It sounds simple, but it's really more like planning and conducting a one-day professional football season. Or a war.

There isn't an enemy in the shipping-day war, but if there was one it would be the "order buyer." Well, sometimes they are the enemy. The order buyer is supposed to represent two parties, the "producer" (seller) and the "feeder" (buyer), at the same time. Solomon, had he not already been busy being a king, or being wise, could have been an order buyer. But even Solomon, on his best day, would not have been trusted. Not completely. Not by either side in the war, because in order to be fair he would have had to be mildly distrusted by both sides. That's the way it works. That's also why, as a group, order buyers drink and smoke too much, drive big cars too fast while talking on a cell phone and change wives like the rest of us rotate pickup tires. They are the used-car salesmen of the livestock industry, and, although they function under pressure that a cardiac surgeon would find intolerable, no one likes or even respects them. Why do they do it? Maybe it's the attraction of writing checks for large amounts using someone else's money. I don't know.

The first time I noticed Henry, we were cutting out the cows with the steer calves to go. And Henry didn't quite fit. There were several reasons for this. Most of the calves were black baldies while Henry was one of the few hereford-marked ones. But he, as I said before, was a bit more yellow shade of red, like he maybe had some dairy blood in his pedigree. We hadn't earmarked the steer calves when we branded. We applied, and saved to tally, an "underbit" from each heifer calf—as much for a way to count the number of female calves branded on any particular day as for a permanent ear mark. As each bull calf was castrated, the testicles were saved to be served as calf fries. The "oysters" were also counted, the total divided by two, equaling the number of steer calves branded. Since he was castrated, I knew that he had been branded, but fuzzy as he was, I couldn't find a clear brand on his left hip. He was also a pretty sorry calf—the kind that looked as if he hadn't had a hot lunch program at his school and his mamma was too busy to pack his lunch bucket before she went to work.

Come to find out, things for Henry were even tougher than I had originally imagined, because he kept sharing lunch with other calves, and not at Henry's mother's house because Henry didn't have a mother. Henry, as the local dimwit Hersheld would sadly say, was "Jist a pore liddle orfink, garsh." However, he was adept at sneaking in to dine while another calf sucked. If the cow suspected that she was serving an uninvited guest, she would reach around to sniff the dinner guest, and since Henry was in the back seat, so to speak, he was often undetected by the smell test. If he was caught, the unwilling hostess kicked the hell out of him and he went on to the next unsuspecting volunteer. It was a tough life, but he had survived.

But because of fate and his departed mamma, life had not treated Henry fairly. He was a few notches below "pretty sorry." On a scale of ten he would probably rate a three. Which is not to say that he did not have value. In fact, he was perfect in one respect.

When receiving cattle for the ultimate owner, who is not there (I don't *know* where he is . . . getting the corn in, seeding the wheat, buying a new pair of suspendered hammer-looped overalls . . . I don't know), the order buyer feels compelled to "cut a few back." It makes no difference how carefully the seller has already culled; it makes no difference that there will be fewer calves change hands than the contract specifies; it makes no difference if the trucks are inefficiently loaded to less than weight capacity. The order buyer will "cut a few back" because "they don't quite fit." It's just something they do in order to earn the right to write those big checks, I guess.

So a few submarginal cattle must be included or the whole deal will be soured. Are you up to speed on this? It works this way: the feeder doesn't want any cattle that won't "work" for him. He expects the order buyer to be his agent and to be on the lookout for the dying, diseased, disabled and unspecified "dinks" that producers are known to attempt to foist off on farmer/feeders. The order buyer needs to be able to report on his cell phone as he red-lines his Eldorado down the road, "Charlie? Dexter. Got three pots headed yer way. Nice calves. Real clean. A little under a hunered 'n' fifty thousan" (weight, not dollars). "Well, I knew you din't want none of them fuzzy, beaver-tailed dinks. Oh, I don' know, probly ten head er so. Well, yah, he bitched some, but you know how these ranchers are. You'll like the calves. Call me when they git there. Bye."

The rancher understands that protocol requires him to haul a few calves away from the scale. Henry was a perfect "cut back." Except it didn't quite work out as I had expected.

There are several games that the buyer and the producer can play on shipping day. Most of them involve "shrink," which is a struggle over how full (of liquid, or dry, or semidry material) the cattle are, as they are weighed. The longer a calf has been off his mother and the more it is choused, stressed, milled, frightened and confused, the more it will shrink . . . up to a point of actual dehydration. The more shrink, the less weight; the less weight, the cheaper the calf, since they are sold by the pound. (I don't know anything about hogs except that they will eat coal. I didn't know that until an order buyer [who shall for obvious reasons remain nameless] told me about letting hogs eat coal prior to going to market to artificially, and temporarily, increase their weight. He said, "You'd be *amazed* how much coal a hog will eat, but you better be long gone when it comes out the other end, 'cause nothin' makes a buyer madder than paying good money for a bunch of black water . . . if you know what I mean.")

One of the shrink games is to "balance the scale." As cattle are weighed, a bit of the semisolid shrink will be deposited on the scale platform. If the scale is not balanced periodically, the buyer keeps rebuying the same manure again and again. Balancing the scale is legitimate. But there is a narrow line here. If the buyer is slowing down the weighing process excessively by balancing too often, or taking too much time doing it while cattle are waiting to be weighed, this is not legitimate. As I said, it's a narrow line.

While the buyer and I were balancing the scale, a truckload that included Henry was just off the scale waiting to be weighed. "Waterbelly!" the order buyer shouted. "That yaller bucket of fuzz is crankin' his tail. See him? Cut that sumbitch out!" Sure enough, Henry was suffering from having a very painful kidney stone lodged in his urethra and was announcing his discomfort to the world by arching his back, stomping his hind feet like an extremely agitated and spoiled two-year-old human child demanding "more candy" and wringing his tail. And rather than weighing the bunch and then weighing him back, he was cut out and put in a side pen and therefore did not cross the scale.

There are a couple of pieces of paper that accompany the calves on the semi trucks to their new home. One is the brand inspection certificate; the other is the health certificate.

After being weighed, a state-approved Brand Inspector examines each calf for a brand in order to insure that only the owner's calves are included in the sale. If there is any doubt, the suspect animal is isolated, restrained, and checked to assure the presence and location of a brand, and therefore the ownership of the calf, before the inspection certificate is completed and the cattle loaded onto the trucks.

A state-licensed veterinarian also examines the calves prior to issuing a certificate of general good health. This is generally regarded as a farce. The order buyer has already visually checked them for health. The rancher has done the same. *Blind* veterinarians could make wages in the fall issuing health certificates. The local vet is usually aware of any local health problems in general and with any problems in a particular ranch's herd. But it is more of a certified vet income program than a guarantee that any bunch of cattle are in good health. It's not the vets' fault, but as I said before, it is pretty much a farce.

Henry Stokke, DVM, was at the stockyards walking through the calves prior to writing the "health" when he saw this "pore liddle orfink, garsh" standing all alone stomping his feet, ringing his tail, and arching his back. "What's the deal on this calf?" Dr. Stokke asked.

"He's got waterbelly," I said.

"I know that," the good doctor replied. "Whatcha gonna do with him?"

"Take him home and let him die, I guess."

"I could operate on him if I had some help," says the Doc. "We could go partners on him, butcher him next fall and split the beef, if you want to."

"Go ahead," I said, then added to a cluster of underemployed neighbors/truck drivers who were lurking around waiting for my wife to show up with the lunch and speculating on what the calves' average weight was, "Why don't some of you guys help the doc work on that calf?"

I suppose you realize that we are fast approaching that part that I warned you about earlier. You could either quit now, or just skip the next couple of paragraphs. They probably aren't even a *necessary* part of the story. Really.

Still with me I see. Well . . .

The first thing we should handle is the anesthesia part. It's similar to the current "Don't ask. Don't tell" policy. I didn't ask and Dr. Stokke didn't say, but I just *assume* some sort of anesthesia was used. But (and this is a big one) even if no painkiller was used, I am of the firm opinion that the calf was suffering such pain from a kidney stone and a soon-to-burst bladder that any pain associated with the operation was minimal, and of short duration, compared with that which the poor beast was suffering from the "condition."

You still have time to quit. Okay? Okay.

The urethra leaves the bladder on a north-facing steer headed southwest, sort of, under the rectum for a ways, then goes down between and fairly close to the surface skin between the nether cheeks, so to speak. Then, right about where the hind legs sprout, or fork away from the torso, there is a pretty tight S curve in the hose and this is where the stone usually lodges. Once the urethra is found in the butt crease between the anus and where the scrotum used to be (remember we are talking about a steer here), a technician can follow it down to the S curve and usually feel the stone through the wall of the tube, which is about the size of a lady's little finger. Upon finding the stone, a slit can be made in the tube, the stone removed, the slit stitched closed and the incision sewn shut as well. This is a pretty obvious solution, but it is *not* the way to do it because scarring will take place at the location of the slit, another stone will be washed downstream and we'll be back where we started—more pain, smaller-caliber tube, risk of burst bladder, etc., and ultimately a slow, agonizing death.

The best way to deal with the problem, and the alternative taken by the good Dr. Henry Stokke, was to do a partial sex change operation where, instead of the ureter continuing down and back up north to the center of the belly, it is severed and a stub of it is brought out through the hide somewhere below the anus, a bit below where a heifer does wee wee from, if you get what I mean.

As a result of the operation, several results resulted: 1) the calf lived. 2) Due, in part, to the nature of the operation, and part in respect for the surgical skill of the practicing doctor, the calf acquired the name of "Henry the Hermaphrodite." 3) Henry, perhaps his bovine brain realizing that people could eliminate pain, elected to become a pet. And 4) Henry urinated in a disgusting and unsanitary manner. Further, although this had less to do with the operation than the fact that he was orphaned too soon in life, Henry, despite all of the feed he consumed, never did prosper. In fact, he was a living example of the bovine silk purse rule: "once a dink, always a dink."

A couple of years went by. One day Dr. Stokke asked me whatever happened to our beef deal. Before thinking, I replied, "Oh, you mean Henry."

"Who?" the doc asked. So I had to tell him the whole story, including, unfortunately, the namesake part. I concluded that I didn't want any part of eating Henry the Hermaphrodite, who forever reeked of the stale urine that soaked his hind legs, irrigated his tail and by switching said tail, managed to lave most of his bony body. In an attempt to make the best of a no-win situation, I proposed shipping the bovine Henry for whatever meager sum he might bring and splitting the proceeds with his sex-change doctor. Dr. Henry agreed.

I'll bet you think that's the end of the story. Oh, no. H the H wasn't finished with us quite yet.

The next time I got a bunch of culls and rejects together to ship to the local sale yard and auction barn, I contacted the local brand inspector because a brand inspection certificate was required before crossing from here, in Rosebud, to Custer County, where the sale yard was located. "What's the story on that sorry, yellow two-year old, or is he a yearling?" brand inspector Bradley asked.

"That's Henry," I told him.

"I know *who* he is. What's the story on the brand?"

"What brand?" I asked.

"That's what I mean," Bradley said. "I don't see the brand."

"That's Henry, for petesake," I said. "Surely you remember him."

"Remember him? I do. See his brand? I don't. Let's run him in the squeeze chute and clip him," Bradley said. So we did. Guess what? No brand on the left hip where my brand is supposed to be. Guess what else? Once we got all the fuzz clipped off, he had a great big QUARTER CIRCLE H on his right rib. A brand neither of us knew. We had never seen it before.

"Why didn't you figure out he wasn't my calf when we shipped a couple of years ago?" I asserted.

"Never looked at him. You guys cut him back before he crossed the scale. Never looked at him."

"Well what the hell we gonna do now?"

"We're gonna find out who he belongs to, I'd say," he says. So we ship the rest of the culls. Henry stays in the corral. On feed. Softly mooing at me through the fence, wanting company.

Four days later Bradley calls, "Henry the Hermaphrodite belongs to a guy clear up at Ryegate."

"What do I do now?" I ask.

"Call him and explain why you've been doing perverted things to his stock without his permission, I guess." I get the idea Bradley is enjoying this. So I call the guy. Come to find out, he summered some cows across Tongue River from our outfit a couple of years before. We figured out one of his cows must have crossed the river with her calf but that only the cow had a round-trip ticket. She left Henry on our side of the river.

I shipped Henry. The rightful owner got the sale proceeds. I paid Henry the vet for the sex-change operation. I could have charged a grazing fee from the owner from Ryegate but I was too embarrassed at my close brush with being a thief.

All the neighbors got a good laugh. Once in a while someone will ask, "Remember Henry the Hermaphrodite? . . . " and sort of let the question fade to black. Sonsabitches.